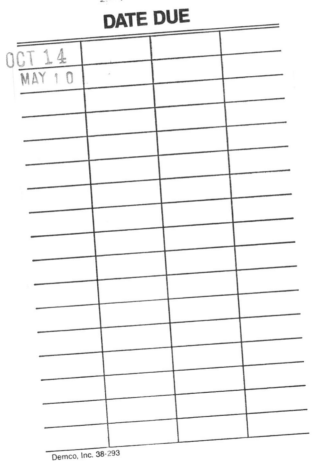

Controlling the Sword

Controlling the Sword

The Democratic Governance of National Security

Bruce Russett

Harvard University Press
Cambridge, Massachusetts
London, England
1990

Library of Congress Cataloging-in-Publication Data

Russett, Bruce M.
  Controlling the sword : the democratic governance
of national security / Bruce Russett.
      p.   cm.
  Includes bibliographical references.
  ISBN 0-674-16990-5 (alk. paper)
  1. Civil-military relations—United States.
  2. Civil-military relations.
  3. United States—Military policy.
  4. United States—Politics and government—1945–
  5. Public opinion—United States.
  6. Democracy.   I. Title.
UA23.R886   1990
322′.5—dc20   89-48851
                                                   CIP

For Robert Dahl and Karl Deutsch
who care about science
and about people

Acknowledgments

In conducting the research I have benefited from financial support from the National Academy of Sciences and the National Research Council, the United States Institute of Peace, the World Society Foundation (Switzerland), the Carnegie Corporation of New York, and the John D. and Catherine T. MacArthur foundation. I am grateful to these institutions for their assistance, but of course they bear no responsibility for the product. I completed the manuscript as a Fulbright Hays research fellow at Tel Aviv University, and I thank both the U.S.–Israel Educational Foundation for the award and my colleagues in Political Science at Tel Aviv for their gracious hospitality and intellectual stimulation. Gad Barzilai, Richard Brody, Robert Dahl, Lloyd Dumas, Lloyd Etheredge, Raymond Gastil, Ole Holsti, David Lumsdaine, Scott Plous, Thomas Risse-Kappen, Robert Shapiro, James Sutterlin, Edward Tufte, Rafi Ventura, Bradford Westerfield, and Burns Weston made helpful comments on part or all of the manuscript.

The earlier work was done at Yale University, much of it in a large-scale project on public opinion and national security conducted as part of the International Security and Arms Control Program. My colleague Thomas W. Graham codirected the project; I am indebted both to his extensive scholarship on this topic and to our many valuable conversations. William Foltz, my colleague of many years, provided key support for the Security and Arms Control Program in general, and for my activities in particular. Several students served as research assistants in various capacities; they include Lisa Brandes, Jonathan Cowden, Thomas Hartley, David Kinsella, George Randels, Erik Ringmar, Jeffrey Small, and Steve Wellman. I also want to express my appreciation for the excellent editorial work by Aida Donald, Camille Smith, and Elizabeth Suttell. An earlier version of Chapter 5 appeared as "A More Democratic and Therefore More Peaceful World," *World Futures* 26 (1990); permission for the use of that material here was granted by Gordon and Breach, Inc.

December 1989

Contents

The man who wears the shoe knows best that it pinches and where it pinches, even if the expert shoemaker is the best judge of how the trouble is to be remedied.

John Dewey, *The Public and Its Problems*

1

Opportunities, Constraints, and Temptations

I believe that ambitious men in democracies are less
engrossed than any others with the interests and the
judgment of posterity; the present moment alone
absorbs them. They are more apt to complete a number
of undertakings with rapidity than to raise lasting monu-
ments to their achievements; and they care more
for success than for fame.

Alexis de Tocqueville, *Democracy in America*

Public opinion, operating in democratic political systems,
shapes and constrains national security policy: the use of military force in the world, the content of nuclear strategy, the
possibilities for arms control and disarmament, the likelihood
of long-term peaceful relations with the Soviet Union. For
elected leaders (and those who try to keep them in office, and
those who would take their places) foreign and security policy
is, in large degree, domestic politics. In a democracy, the political
leader who ignores domestic politics hamstrings his or her ability to get things done internationally, risks repudiation domestically, and ignores a set of resources—real or symbolic successes
abroad—that could help bring success at home also.

This book suggests how different leaders' successes and failures in comprehending the constraints imposed by democratic
political systems have contributed to those leaders' ability to
achieve foreign policy goals, and in turn how the success and
failure of foreign policy have enhanced or sabotaged leaders'
ability to achieve their domestic policy goals. Using information
from public opinion surveys, systematic studies of political processes, and illustrations from the policy world, the book shows,
for example, how electoral politics encourage tough talk and
tough action toward adversaries, but more by some kinds of

leaders than by others; how policymaking and public opinion interact, with opinion sometimes influencing and other times being manipulated by policymakers; how the public balances extremes of warmongering and appeasement in a centripetal manner; how democratic political systems are readier to compromise their differences with countries which also are democratically governed, and virtually never go to war against other democracies.

The book also debunks several myths often invoked to justify antidemocratic efforts to keep national security policymaking tightly controlled by elites: myths that the general public is too ignorant of and confused about national security issues to deserve influence over policy; that the public is too easily manipulated; that public opinion is volatile, swinging irrationally between indifference and hysteria, or between the postures of hawk and chicken. It shows not just the difficulty, but the possibility and the necessity, of involving the public in creating and sustaining a sensible national security policy for a democratic country.

It is primarily a book about national security policy in the American political system, one of the two political systems that have the greatest influence over whether our descendants will live to welcome the twenty-second century. But we cannot understand the American political system without also comprehending how it is similar to or different from other political systems, especially other democratically governed countries. Hence the book makes substantial use of material from other democratic countries as well. The opening chapter is painted in broad-brush style without the accoutrements of scholarly references; subsequent chapters include citations to the social scientific literature, but presented in a nontechnical manner.

The social-scientific material is composed most prominently of data from public opinion surveys, but the questions addressed go beyond what can primarily be answered by survey information. Thus another large piece comprises the literature on how the state of the economy and domestic politics interact, extending some of those ideas and findings to foreign policy. The book also reviews some major issues in contemporary international relations theory, and explores some crucial questions about the circumstances in which democracies may be more or less peaceful than differently governed states, including questions about how democracies behave toward one another. All this material is integrated here into a comprehensive effort at understanding what makes the system tick.

The social-scientific review material is interspersed with illustrative case information on the behavior of policymakers, and how they interpret and use the information they have on public opinion. Both kinds of materials can be instructive—the cases for illustrating and refining rather than for "proving" the generalizations—though they are not often used together in work on public opinion. Jointly they form the basis for an interpretive essay on the contribution of public opinion to shaping policy.

A Tale of Two Presidents

Not every elected leader is treated equally kindly by domestic politics or, more important, is equally skilled in understanding and using domestic politics as he goes about the business of foreign policy. The two most recent American presidencies illustrate this well.

Jimmy Carter's inaugural address included a brave call for "the elimination of all nuclear weapons from this earth," and he began his administration with a bold new strategic arms proposal to the leaders of the Soviet Union. Ronald Reagan, by contrast, campaigned against the "fatally flawed" SALT II agreement, resisted pressures for a nuclear freeze, and spent the first six years of his administration building up American military strength and avoiding any arms control pact. Yet Carter's SALT II agreement remained unratified, and his arms control initiatives—like much of the rest of his one-term presidency—failed. Reagan, by contrast, achieved overwhelming approval for a major nuclear *disarmament* (not just arms control) agreement, the Intermediate-range Nuclear Forces (INF) treaty eliminating some weapons in Europe, and helped set in motion a wide-ranging and promising thaw in relations with the Soviet Union. Why did one fail while the other not only succeeded but succeeded in a direction quite opposite from that to which his initial policies and apparent predispositions pointed?

Many factors conspired against Carter and in favor of Reagan. Consider some of the ways in which the last two years of their presidencies differed. Jimmy Carter began as a Washington "outsider," and neither he nor many of his staff ever really learned to deal effectively with the power brokers in Congress or the federal bureaucracy. He achieved his presidency with a narrow electoral victory and within fifteen months his approval rating in the country at large ("Do you approve of the way [Jimmy Carter] is handling his job as President?") had fallen to only 40 percent. Several times in his last two years it dropped below 30 percent.

Carter presided over a time of economic troubles: the consumer price index inflated at a rate of 12.5 percent over each of the last two years of his presidency, and per capita real income, after rising only 1 percent in 1979, in 1980 fell back to the 1978 level. Much of the fault lay in the shock of oil price increases for which he was not responsible; nevertheless economic discontent was widespread at the time when he sought reelection. A president is expected to deliver two items to the electorate: peace and prosperity. The second was slipping badly, and so too was the first.

In the first two years of his presidency Carter was widely perceived as a dove. He spent a large share of his political capital to achieve ratification of an internationally necessary but domestically unpopular treaty returning control of the Panama Canal to the government of Panama. He began trying to salvage an already fading détente with the Soviet Union, but events overwhelmed him. Soviet arms procurement pressed steadily ahead while that of the United States at first languished. American- and Soviet-supplied client states battled around the world. Ethiopia fought Somalia, and according to Zbigniev Brzezinski, Carter's National Security Adviser, détente was "buried in the sands of the the Ogadan" desert in East Africa. If not there, it was lost in the jungles of Angola, the villages of Nicaragua, and the mountains of Afghanistan. Soviet leader Leonid Brezhnev, in declining health, was neither able nor inclined to improve the international climate. Feeling betrayed, Carter became more of a hawk, but too late to save his public image.

On top of this, events in Iran, for which the Soviet Union was not responsible, proved a disaster. Carter could not negotiate release of the hostages, and a high-risk effort to free them by military action collapsed when the helicopters didn't work. Cynics so widely anticipated that he might try again for a military rescue—of the hostages and his declining presidency—with an "October surprise" that it became politically impossible. He went to the election with the television sounds and images of demonstrating Iranian "students" steadily before the voters. Once ratification of SALT II was delayed into 1979 and 1980 the treaty was lost, as was any other arms control agreement such as a comprehensive nuclear test ban.

Ronald Reagan, by contrast, won the presidency by a substantial margin of votes. By "good fortune" he was shot early in 1981, and public sympathy pushed his approval rating up almost to 70 per cent. In the reelection campaign Walter Mondale was doomed from the start and Reagan won by a landslide. Even after the initial damage of the Iran-Contra scandal in late 1986, Reagan's approval rating hovered around 50 percent, unusually high for any president so late in his term of office. His personal popularity ("everyone's favorite grandfather") remained high even as his image of competence and control evaporated.

After a brief recession in 1981 and 1982, the economy went into an unprecedentedly long period of prosperity and stable prices. The taming of inflation was due as much to the Federal Reserve and to the collapse of OPEC as to any fiscal wisdom of the administration, and of course the prosperity was bought at the price of enormous deficits in the federal budget and the country's international balance of payments. Many observers could see the day of reckoning looming, but it did not appear during Reagan's days in office. People might have felt a malaise about the economic future, but the Reagan administration maintained the surface condition of prosperity in good shape.

In foreign policy, Reagan campaigned as a hawk. He vowed to scrap arms control agreements, like SALT, that he called one-sided to America's disadvantage, and to rebuild American military strength. In office, he proceeded to do both. He provided aid to "freedom fighters" against communist governments around the world, aid that in some places—Afghanistan especially, perhaps also Angola and Cambodia, though not in Nicaragua—was more productive than even most members of the administration expected. With an effective if hardly militarily efficient invasion Reagan overthrew the Marxist government of Grenada. He even rejected a proffered arms control agreement in Europe—to forgo installing Pershing missiles in exchange for sharp cuts in Soviet deployment of intermediate-range missiles—that his own negotiator, Paul Nitze, then considered a good deal. His gift for popular exposition, coupled with a highly competent staff of speechwriters and a sophisticated polling operation able to advise what policies would be popular and how to package them symbolically, retained public acquiescence and, in large part, enthusiasm.

By his second term, however, Reagan and some members of his administration began to show more interest in arms control and in a warmer political relationship with the Soviet Union. Mikhail Gorbachev, for his own reasons, was ready to oblige. When the Iranian arms scandal emerged at the end of that year, the Reagan presidency was gravely weakened. The press not only exposed the harebrained policy but began to expose how little the president apparently knew or even cared about what his nominal subordinates had been doing.[1] The Reagan administration, well into lame-duck status, badly needed a success, somewhere. With a Democratic Congress able to block any serious further fulfillment of Reagan's domestic economic and social agenda, foreign policy was the obvious candidate. Thanks to his credentials as a hawk, he could gain speedy and overwhelming ratification of a good INF agreement, and go off to Moscow proclaiming the reformation of the "evil empire." Yet by some lights, what is remarkable about the concrete arms control accomplishments of Reagan's last two years is that they were so meagre. Chances for a 50 percent reduction in strategic arms or a test ban treaty were sacrificed for the president's chimeric Star Wars notion. He chose not to go beyond the INF treaty, which, however much he may have believed in it for itself, not coincidentally served his domestic political goals well.

It is striking how overdetermined both of these two cases of national security policy failure and success seem. With the wisdom of hindsight it is hard to imagine how Jimmy Carter could have succeeded in his aims, or how Ronald Reagan could have

1. The administration did some polling on whether the president looked better if he was perceived as aware of and responsible for the policy, or if the policy was perceived to have been carried out by subordinates without his knowledge. The result was a public posture that the president was in charge of policy generally but had not authorized the specific illegal actions.

failed in his. The state of the economy, exigencies of domestic politics, the image of leadership and foreign policy preferences that each brought to office, the respective popularity and communication skills (or lack thereof) of the two presidents, and world events all pointed to the same conclusions. One can hardly say which of these factors was more important, and perhaps none was essential to the outcome. But together they produced it.

Another aspect of this compilation of forces is how many of them represent dimensions of domestic rather than international politics, despite the fact that one imagines national security policy is designed to achieve particular results in dealings with other nations. The success or failure of international policy is in fact substantially driven by domestic political developments, and so, therefore, is the choice of policy by a leader who aspires to success. Policies of arms control and disarmament, negotiation or threat, conciliation or the use of military force are adopted in large part because they gratify friends and disarm adversaries at home, not because they necessarily seem sensible in some abstract principle of the national interest abroad. Furthermore, the political horizon shaping those decisions is typically a short one, not a vision for the long haul.

The Triangle of Forces on Foreign Policy

Foreign policy, of any sort, emerges from the interplay of a variety of forces. The top echelon of the executive branch charged with deciding and directing the execution of major items of foreign policy is subject to, and in turn influences, three sets of other actors. Figure 1.1 presents those influences on an American president in a simple fashion.

Most obviously, the top leadership operates in the world beyond its national borders. It tries to effect change in that world (or, perhaps, to resist change and perpetuate the status quo), and in turn is affected by the outside world. It encounters external actors (states, international organizations, multinational corporations based abroad, terrorist organizations) which it cannot influence at an acceptable cost, and it is subject to the efforts of those actors to influence its own behavior. There are limits to its own power, and other international actors have their own

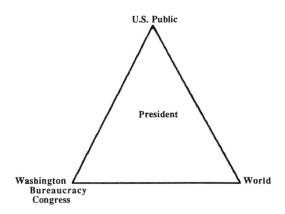

Figure 1.1. The triangle of forces within which the United States president operates in foreign policy.

sources of active power in turn. Some of these actors are more or less reliable friends or allies, others are frequent adversaries. But they all have their own goals and resources with which to pursue those goals. Their action or inaction feeds back to the American political system along legs of the triangle—especially to the public directly as in the form of higher prices or defense costs—as well as to the president himself. The United States has been, for most of this century, uniquely powerful in the range of resources it can bring to bear on others; it is less constrained by its external environment than is almost any other nation. Nevertheless, even the United States must recognize limits and the potential or actual influence of others, and adjust its behavior accordingly. A contemporary president needs the cooperation of other nations, as allies, as trade partners, or even as adversaries with whom it is necessary to limit conflcts and control arms.

Foreigners, however, do not vote. Foreign policy decisionmakers are heavily influenced by the domestic political environment in which they operate; indeed, to the degree that external constraints on the United States are relatively weak, the domestic constraints are relatively stronger than for the leaders of other governments. They may even be absolutely stronger. Constitutionally, the American executive is weaker than that of many other governments. Operating in a federal system, many objects of attention are beyond its direct reach, in the hands of state and local governments. At the federal level, the separation of powers constrains it. Washington is full of people with their own bases of power and with much experience in using their power. Members of Congress may sometimes be told what to do, but much more often they must be cajoled, conciliated, bargained with. The vast federal bureauracy is nominally under the president's control, but entrenched bureacratic interests and organizational perspectives, the realities of complex politics, and the civil service structure all contribute to an ability to resist the impact of directives from the top. Franklin Roosevelt likened the Department of the Navy to a feather pillow; John Kennedy the State Department to a bowl of jello. In turn, those interests, perspectives, and politics influence the kinds of information that members of the bureaucracy send up to their top leaders; the overburdened leadership receives only a tiny and by no means unbiased fraction of the information that has passed through multiple screens along the way.

How Domestic Politics Matter

Perhaps most important, the top leadership is constrained by the fact that it works in a relatively open, democratic political system. Leaders may try to insulate their decisions from direct popular control, and their ability to do so varies over time and, especially, with the issue at hand. Some of their best opportunities to insulate their actions from domestic politics occur in the realm of foreign and national security policy. Foreign policy issues, especially those concerned with peace and war, are generally acknowledged to be complex, often requiring technical expertise and a range of hard-to-get, often clandestinely acquired information. Nuclear strategy has especially been the preserve of an elite "priesthood" of expertise—ironically, because nowhere else could errors affect Americans so devastatingly.

In general on foreign policy matters, the president and his immediate subordinates are assumed to have unusual access to expertise and information; they are often given the benefit of the doubt, and outsiders may be reluctant to challenge their judgments. Outsiders may simply be wrong and, perhaps worse, may be shown to be wrong by a president who wishes to draw on what he has been told by his advisers. Furthermore, there is the image of the president as "president of all the people"; he is enshrined as the embodiment of the national interest, the one who is at the apex of political pressures as well as that of the national information network, and so best represents the national interest. That he has his own interests—as an individual, as a partisan, as a member of a class—is not forgotten, but he is at least theoretically in the best position to surmount them or to integrate them into the mystical "national interest."

The president must nevertheless care, intensely, about how popular he and his policies are in the country at large. He is at the peak of a system in which innumerable interest groups compete for attention and influence, sometimes operating alone, usually in shifting coalitions with other groups. These groups "command" (that's the wrong word, because they too are subject to many vectors of influence) financial resources, media sympathy, and votes. In a democracy, votes do in some sense matter. Maybe not every day or on every issue, but no elected official can ignore the process by which he or she originally obtained electoral approval or the ease with which that approval can evaporate in response to a perception that the leader has not been sufficiently responsive to the vox of particular populi. A political leader must worry about his or her next election, or that of the heir apparent, and the public image of continuing electoral popularity and hence power. Members of Congress as well as the chief executive must care about public attitudes, including attitudes on foreign policy. They may not wish or be able to please all the people all of the time, but they must satisfy some important subset of their constituents and funders. If they cannot satisfy demands, they must try to explain why the course they are following is correct. (Note the influence relationships along this side of the triangle, as well as between the public and the president.)

A popular leader can convince adversaries that they are dealing with someone who will be around for some time; someone who has the ability to deliver the goods well into the future and someone who, if alienated, can unleash political resources against adversaries. Popularity gets or keeps a politician in office, and the continuing image of popularity heavily influences how effective he or she will be while in office. Popularity may be gained or lost by foreign policy actions taken in the name of the president, or by actions taken by foreign leaders to reward or punish the United States. It may also be gained or lost by actions or events in domestic politics, seemingly far removed from foreign affairs: by the state of the economy, or by the demands of interest groups for social legislation. Insofar as responses to these acts affect the general public's perception that the president is or is not "doing a good job," his power in foreign affairs is enhanced or diminished.

A decision about foreign policy may therefore be affected by actors at any of the points of the triangle and, equally important, may be intended to retain or strengthen the president's power at any of those points. Foreign policy actions are ostensibly directed at actors in the external world, but in fact that may be so only nominally. A president may impose a grain embargo less to influence the Soviet Union than to impress voters at home with his toughness against a militarily active foreign adversary; a subsequent president may repeal the embargo far less because it has achieved its stated foreign policy purpose than because he needs the domestic political support of growers and shippers of grain, and of members of Congress from their states. He may embark on a summit meeting less because he expects to reach a substantively important agreement than because it is good domestic politics to be seen negotiating with—but not appeasing—the leader of another great power. He may choose to launch an air strike against Libya less because he expects to eliminate Libyan terrorism than because he needs to be seen, by his domestic constituents, to be doing something to combat international terrorists.

This does not imply that a president acts solely or even primarily with the exigencies of domestic politics in mind. Surely he does take his role as president of all the people to heart. Surely he knows that a record of long-run failure in foreign policy, attributable to actions that maximized his short-run political interests at home, will eventually come back to punish him in domestic politics as well. But it is rarely fully clear what will be a success and what a failure in foreign policy, or how to achieve success (is peace best preserved by toughness or conciliation?), and one may delude oneself as well as others. And as Lord Keynes said, "in the long run we are all dead." The temptation to pursue short-run gains, and either not to take account of the long or simply to hope for the best, is always present, and presidents are not immune to it. Votes or popularity points lost today mean a weakened ability to achieve goals tomorrow; next year can be worried about when and if it arrives.

The relative importance of these different influences varies over time, and especially over the course of a president's term in office. During his first hundred days, or perhaps his first year, his popularity is highest and his accumulation of enemies lowest. He has a chance to do a few big things if he can do them quickly and decisively. Usually he is more experienced in domestic politics than in foreign policy. (George Bush is the only exception since Dwight D. Eisenhower.) In the big, insular, and still somewhat isolated country that the United States is, domestic policy will affect far more people, and bring the president more rewards or punishments, than will any foreign policy act other than war. His electoral victory has been achieved against domestic political adversaries and has brought allies into domestic political office; it has not affected the power base of his foreign adversaries and negotiating partners. Hence now is the time to deal with the domestic players; the foreigners usually can wait. (Too quick a readiness to act in foreign policy before settling in can lead to disaster, as it did for John Kennedy at the Bay of Pigs.)[2]

So the combination of his experience and his incentives brings him to concentrate his efforts on the home front. Then he may turn to foreign affairs, but soon the midterm congressional elections are due. He must campaign for his party, trying to hold the inevitable midterm losses to some minimum. His coattails for this are very short, although a well-orchestrated summit meeting or other success in foreign policy may help a little bit. By the third year scandals have begun to emerge and some of his appointees begin to leave, or should leave. If it is his first term in office he must begin to position himself for the reelection campaign, and in the fourth year devote his attention wholeheartedly to it. Again, some kinds of foreign policy actions—bold ones, achiev-

---

2. The calendar is not the same for a vice president assuming the presidency without an election. He typically retains, at least for a while, most of his predecessor's team, and likely will choose substantial continuity in domestic policy. He may, however, feel a need to demonstrate his resolve in foreign affairs. Truman with the Russians, Johnson in Vietnam, and Ford in the Mayaguez affair all suggest the pressures of such a need.

ing the image if not necessarily the substance of short-term success—will repay him. But with the election in mind, much of foreign policy is only a diversion, or worse a danger if the obstreperous foreigners prove unmanageable. The state of the economy and its impact on his electoral prospects must be his first priority. If it is not good, a short-term foreign policy success may be worth something to turn attention away from economic adversity, but likely it will be little more than a consolation prize.

The second term in office begins as something of a replay of the first, in that the president has a new and often more impressive electoral mandate. He and his team also have the benefit of four years' experience, and probably some solid achievements in domestic affairs. The new term therefore offers him a chance for some more achievements, and the chance to shift his focus somewhat toward foreign policy. The early part of this term is his last good chance to reach goals that he himself primarily defines. After that, the constraints close in. He is a lame duck, whose ability to promise rewards or punishments very far into the future has vanished. Everyone knows he cannot deliver much in the midterm elections, or even transfer much of his popularity to his successor. By the last two years many of his appointees are leaving, he has lost support in another midterm election, and everyone's attention is on the next round of presidential nomination and election. His ability to promote major policy initiatives in domestic politics has slipped away. Foreign policy may seem to hold his best remaining opportunities, but even there his success is dependent partially on his ability to communicate to foreign leaders that he has the domestic political support to deliver on his promises, and many of those promises require explicit congressional approval or appropriation. He therefore can do things in foreign policy, but, possibly more than ever before, he must choose from a menu of actions that will be popular at home. This menu may not be the one he started with, and he may feel like a customer in a very different restaurant. Once the election is over he can only wait until January 20.

Thus there are stages in the electoral cycle within which the incentive and capability to act effectively in foreign policy vary greatly. The best opportunity to achieve something is probably at the beginning of his first term, but the incentive—overwhelmed as he is by the need to master the system and achieve something in domestic politics—is lacking. Later in the term he can turn more of his attention to foreign policy, but his ability to gather domestic support for his actions suffers ups and downs. The best confluence of incentive and support probably comes at the beginning of his second term, if he ever gets to it. But that too fades quickly enough. By the latter part of the second term he is reduced to doing things that will be popular, not necessarily what he would have chosen in light of his earlier preferences and agenda. He has done all that he could do out of that agenda; what he can do at the end is only the unexpected, shifting his ground and co-opting his domestic political adversaries by adopting some of their policies in ways they cannot then oppose.

Other Democratic Political Systems

The U.S. commander-in-chief faces a particular set of constraints and temptations imposed by domestic politics, made especially acute by the presidential system, which weakens his control over the legislature and thus drives him to try to rally popular support behind his program. But leaders of other nations, often operating in very different political systems—presidential, parliamentary, federal, unitary, mildly dictatorial, vigorously repressive—in prosperous and parlous economies, and with populations that are variously satisfied, restive, or outright rebellious, have their own limitations. Their cycles of constraint and opportunity, whether bound to their electoral calendars or to their own health and that of conspirators against them, rarely coincide with his. A window of opportunity that seems open to him may be closed to them, whatever their basic intentions.

This sketch of leadership politics is drawn from the experience of domestic and foreign policy in the United States, and the book will proceed to document and elaborate many of the propositions from which it is constructed. But while primarily directed toward the United States and illustrated by American materials, the book will also use material from other democratic political systems. There are some important similarities, although the particular configuration of checks and balances in the United States will not be found elsewhere, nor will the combination of national power and insulation that produces the great influence of domestic politics in the United States. In less "privileged" political systems the room for manuever in dealing with other countries is narrower, and the ability to give primacy to domestic politics without risking international disaster is much less.

Swedish leaders may face many similar domestic political constraints, but both they and their constituents know they must take much greater care in talking tough to their Soviet neighbor or in threatening to use military force. Other countries, such as the Netherlands, may have more favorable geopolitical situations than Sweden, but like the Swedes may have given up ambitions to imperial or global status. Perhaps sheltered under the umbrella of an alliance, they need not pursue active adversarial relations with any other states. Their incentives to talk tough or use military force are minimal. They most often react to the actions of others, and once they have settled on a basic foreign policy stance such as alignment or nonalignment they may have little room for major initiatives. Still others, such as Japan, have willingly or unwillingly renounced both the use of force and the acquisition of major military capabilities. They have little military strength either to use or to bargain away.

Some other democratically governed countries do, however, share important elements of the American condition. France and Britain are no longer major powers with the ability to use military force very independently (the French substantially stopped after getting out of Algeria; the British had one more fling over the Falklands), but for a long time they were. We can learn something from looking at their history, especially that of Britain, which was once the predominant world power.

There are also some useful parallels with a much weaker country, Israel. The Israeli multiparty parliamentary system does not create a strong executive, especially in recent years, when no party has seemed able to form a stable government by itself. The system is highly pluralistic and intensely politicized. Public opinion polling is a finely developed art in Israel, and shifts in domestic attitudes and approvals are rapidly detected. Basic consensus is lacking on the means by which to achieve the national goal of survival. There is agreement on the need for a strong military establishment, but not on much of the strategy or tactics for its use or on the territorial shape or form of governance of the system which is to be defended. Arab adversaries pose continual military threats and periodic military actions, but the timing and nature of the Israeli response, or the kinds of initiatives Israel should take, are subject to great disagreement. The Israeli government must take care not to alienate its superpower ally, the United States, but over the years has learned how to manipulate that ally. Hence Israeli leaders too are heavily influenced in their choices by their own domestic politics as well as by what is done to them by foreign actors.

If we include Israel, with its weak executive, and Britain, as a great power over most of the past century, we have the makings of a theory for two and a half countries and, more marginally, for some other democracies as well. The context and the specifics will vary from that of the United States, from which most of the material is drawn.

Using the System

Different leaders, and different American presidents, have different chances to do different things in foreign policy. The coincidence of these chances with the leaders' visions of what they want to do, and their political skills, controls whether they will succeed and what they will succeed at. Some presidents—and some policy advocates who would advise them—will do better than others.

Ronald Reagan produced an arms control/disarmament agreement—limited though it was to intermediate-range nuclear forces—after more liberal leaders had failed. In fact, there had been no significant arms agreement since ratification of the SALT I strategic arms control and ABM (antiballistic missile) treaties in 1972. Richard Nixon was responsible for them. Political activists and government officials of a dovish bent have not achieved a strategic arms control treaty in more than two decades, not since the outer space treaty in 1967 and the partial test ban treaty in 1963. They have won many battles of intellectual analysis, producing proposals that often were technically sophisticated or well suited to international conditions. But they have lost the subsequent domestic wars of political implementation. The political defeats of liberal arms controllers range from the loss of international control of atomic energy in the 1940s, through efforts for a comprehensive test ban in the 1950s and early l960s and the failure to ratify SALT II in the 1970s, to the collapse of the nuclear freeze movement in the early 1980s. Conservative presidents have an inherent political cover when they choose to move left, but their success is due also to their political skill.

One reason liberal advocates of arms control and nuclear reductions have failed is that they have not understood the dynamics of public opinion and its complicated relationship to American politics. Liberal policy analysts and advocates of arms control often assume, in an elitist way, that public opinion is not really relevant; that what matters is producing an objectively good proposal and persuading other members of the national security elite that it is indeed a good proposal. Popular attitudes don't matter much therefore, and perhaps even it is best not to stir up too much public interest, which might be volatile and ill-informed. Or, liberal analysts may simply assume that the people are on the side of peace and arms control. They have rarely asked questions like these: What does the public know about arms control and nuclear weapons? What are their attitudes about arms control, and what are the relationships between attitudes about arms control and other attitudes such as those toward the Soviet Union, the president's job performance, or military spending?

Unfortunately, public attitudes are not simple, and not well understood even by professional analysts. Public support of SALT II was well below the level needed to sustain a two-thirds majority in the Senate. Majorities in the public favor both strength and conciliation; they want negotiations but will often applaud the use of military force; their fear of nuclear war can lead them to support both nuclear arms reductions and the Strategic Defense Initiative (SDI). From the viewpoint of an advocate of arms control, public attitudes are complex and often contradictory.

Wishing to protect its own position as representative of the popular will, the U.S. Congress has restricted the use of public funds for polling by the executive branch, but ways have been found to circumvent the restrictions. Under the Carter administration the Democratic National Committee funded a survey operation out of the White House run by Patrick Cadell. After Reagan was elected that operation was greatly expanded, under the auspices of the Republican National Committee and the direction of Richard Wirthlin. The Reagan administration assembled the most complete and sophisticated capability for evaluating public opinion in the history of the presidency. Its superior knowledge of public opinion and use of the media allowed it to select the timing for its initiatives and to frame the discussion in ways that were most advantageous to its position. Aided by the administration's polling, the White House staff worried about how their actions would be portrayed, and how to word their press releases. Opponents of arms control have been years ahead of its advocates in analyzing and using data on public opinion. If democratic competition is to work well, both sides must know how to play the game.

In its first six years, the Reagan administration began by derogating the wisdom and prudence of previous policies, such as restraint in weapons procurement and the ABM and SALT treaties, and then diverted public concern away from concluding agreements on strategic arms control to being satisfied with the process of negotiations and the prospect of a perfect defense. (Handling of the Reykjavik negotiations in October 1986 is a perfect example. In substance the negotiations collapsed, but the image of a continuing process was maintained, in the context of Reagan's insistence that he would not trade SDI away. Previously the administration had succeeded in making the nuclear freeze movement fade away without conceding any discernible shift in policy.) Even when unplanned events occurred, the White House's detailed knowledge of the pattern of public attitudes and its ongoing survey research effort gave it a huge comparative advantage over its domestic opponents. The 1987 INF agreement was in part an effort by a weakened administration to do something that would be widely popular, but also to shape attitudes for subsequent years with emphasis on the process (for example, of an arms buildup to a "bargaining position of strength," hard bargaining, and retention of SDI) that allegedly produced the agreement. The public "framing" of the INF treaty and the rhetoric of settling for nothing but "deep cuts" will have a continuing impact on American attitudes. The administration was thus acting in international politics, performing for a domestic political audience by invoking particular memories and symbols of past events, and coloring the domestic political perception of reality in order to shape the acts of its successors.

This book is devoted primarily to the impact of international security and arms control policy on public attitudes and perceptions, and reciprocally, the constraints and incentives that public opinion poses for policy ostensibly addressed to international security matters. We shall also be looking at other connections within and along the triangle, but this all too often neglected one will be our primary focus. This is not, for example, a book about legislative-executive relations, or covert operations and the control over access to information within the government itself.

We shall begin by considering how the state of the economy affects the president's popularity and his incentives to be tough or conciliatory in foreign policy. After that we look at a variety of data on public opinion to see the spectrum of "acceptable" political actions, how that spectrum has evolved over the post–World War II era, and how the public's preference for mixed and "centrist" policies rewards leaders for taking actions, within that spectrum, that were not to be anticipated from those leaders' earlier words and acts. Then we turn to the consistency and stability of public opinion, and the difficult problem of what affects what: to what degree does the governing elite control public opinion, and to what degree does public opinion constrain what legislative and executive leaders can safely say and do?

We conclude the examination in two ways. First, we consider the peaceful and bellicose tendencies of democracy in general, and speculate on whether and how greater democratization in countries around the globe would help to make the world less prone to carry on lethal conflicts. Then we review all the material in the book to pull together some observations about the conditions under which various kinds of security policies are likely to be politically acceptable, and about the range of domestic political options within which creative national security leaders may operate. In other words, we begin to understand how a democracy can sustain a sensible security policy.

2

Bashing the Foreigners

Reputation is an idle and most false imposition; oft got without merit, and lost without deserving.

Iago, in *Othello*

Political leaders, especially those in a democracy, live precarious lives: the demands made always exceed the leaders' capacity to satisfy them. Leaders are expected to solve numerous—and contradictory—social problems, to provide employment and prosperity without inflation and peace with strength. Elected officials will in some sense be held responsible for their actions in office. If enough voters are dissatisfied, officials will not be reelected. To prevent voters' dissatisfaction, officials can deliver what the voters want, persuade the voters that they are delivering even if they aren't, persuade the voters not to want what the officials cannot or do not wish to deliver, or distract the voters' attention by creating or dealing with a new problem. All these are tried and true stratagems.

The most straightforward is to deliver what the voters want. Most voters, most of the time, care most about the national pocketbook. Economic conditions form the primary element in voters' decisions about whether to support incumbent politicians. If the economy is expanding, with an inflation rate that is acceptable in its historical context, then the economy will not usually be declared to be a problem. Under most such circumstances the party in power will start with a high level of popular approval, and the burden will fall on the opposition to distract or persuade about something else, to generate voter unrest by referring to other kinds of problems allegedly facing the country. If peace seems endangered, or if a war is currently being fought, then foreign and security policy may become a major issue, perhaps the most important one.[1]

But if the economy is stagnant or in recession, or if inflation is high, voters usually overtly declare that the state of the economy is the country's most important problem. Voters usually will know directly that the government is not delivering and will not easily be persuaded that they don't want greater prosperity. The incumbent political party or coalition will be in trouble, and typically will be forced to distract the voters' attention to other issues or problems, existing or created. Focus on an alleged threat to security is one possibility, which may or may not be effective as a diversion.

In this chapter we shall first look at a variety of theories that associate improvement or deterioration in the state of the economy with incentives for international conflict, including incentives to divert attention from domestic troubles. We then will consider the special case of economic decline in a democratic polity, and relate that to the general phenomenon of using foreign conflicts as a means to rally political support at home. The chapter will conclude with some observations about the long-term political effects of involvement in war.

Economic Theories of International Conflict

Diversionary or scapegoating theories of war are related to an even larger set of theories stressing economic motivations for war. Such theories include those about long-understood motives for imperial conquest stemming from the desire to acquire new lands or raw materials, and Marxist theories of imperialism—and of conflict among imperial powers—as rooted in declining

1. In the continuing series of Gallup (AIPO) polls, economic conditions and foreign affairs usually occupy, in one order or the other, the top two positions when people are asked, "What is the most important problem facing the country today?" Economic conditions have held first place since 1973 with few exceptions; before that foreign affairs were at the top during most of the cold war era, save principally for periods of recession. See Smith, 1985; Schuman, Ludwig, and Krosnick, 1986. Israel, with its especially severe security condition, is an exception; the military, peace, and security form the dominant issues affecting people's sense of well-being. See Stone, 1982.

profits at home and the consequent need to find foreign markets to absorb surplus capital.

One of the most sweeping theories asserts the existence of "long (50–60 year) waves" of expansion and recession in the world economy, with the most destructive wars occurring on the upswing, in periods of prosperity (quite the opposite of what I was suggesting with scapegoat theories). This theory began with the Soviet economist Nikolai Kondratieff in 1925, and has acquired somewhat more substance with a massive recent examination of data covering the period of the last five centuries (Thompson and Zuk, 1982; Mansfield, 1988; esp. Goldstein, 1988). Scholars looking at more recent international wars have developed explanations about the effects of what they call lateral pressures. In periods of global prosperity and expansion, rapidly growing economies and populations demand ever-increasing supplies of raw materials; political leaders of the competing states, acting on behalf of their national economic interests, may come into conflict in an effort to establish spheres of influence, colonies, and secure sources of supplies.

Some see this phenomenon as a key contributor to World War I, with important analogies to the present (Choucri and North, 1975; Ashley, 1980). Fears of an impending economic (and therefore domestic political) breakdown may have contributed to the willingness of German and Austro-Hungarian leaders, in 1914, to accept at least a "small" war and the substantial risk of a very big one, which they got (Mayer, 1977). By a related interpretation, German leaders feared political upheaval resulting from rapid industrialization, and tried to produce domestic cohesion by making international threats and by a search for small triumphs, which in turn aroused fear in other states (Gordon, 1974). But while intriguing, all these theories are addressed to the broad, large-scale movements in international economic expansion and crisis that may shake the very foundations of a regime. They say little or nothing about the likelihood that war or international crisis will be induced by governments' responses to the short-term ups and downs that occur in modern economies within the span of any longer major cycles.

Other investigators have looked at these shorter-term business cycles and their association with war. Some have claimed—as with the so-called long waves—to see a coincidence of wars with the upswing of the business cycle, in moods of optimism and confidence in the ability to control political adventures such as wars (Macfie, 1938; Blainey, 1973). Confidence and optimism may not be the only forces impelling foreign adventures. In 1938 and 1939 the German economy had become badly overheated by rearmament, producing inflation, shortages of goods and labor, and a balance-of-payments deficit. Hitler perhaps felt impelled to strike then, and also before his opponents could rearm (Carr, 1972; Knox, 1984). Systematic analyses of many cases, however, have failed to turn up any evidence for a general pattern of war and economic expansion, outside of long-cycle phenomena (Thompson, 1982).

The opposite hypothesis is perhaps more plausible: economic decline frequently brings international conflict in its wake. Several causal mechanisms may operate. When the economy begins to falter, the government comes under increasing pressure to "do something," among which trade protectionism typically looms large. If tariffs, import quotas, and other means of excluding foreigners' goods are put in place, the effects on other countries are usually contagious and create conflict. The consequence may be a marked decline in international trade, followed by further deterioration in domestic economies and further exacerbation of international political conflicts. The 1930s are widely thought to have exemplified this process (Kindleberger, 1973).

A more important chain may be one that progresses through militarization. Another variant of "do something" is pump-priming to stimulate the domestic economy, and if pump-priming includes military spending it can have significant political consequences. On the one hand, it reinforces the domestic arguments for similar policies in other countries by generating an external stimulus for them, in effect starting an arms race. That is, it can generate higher levels of threat-perception among the political elites in neighboring countries or traditional rivals. What may have begun as a purely internal measure for economic renewal can end up as an international provocation. Furthermore, increases in military spending and recruitment also have effects at home, increasing the political influence of the beneficiaries. The net result of these domestic and international processes will therefore be an increased militarization of the separate nations' foreign policies, and an increased level of international tension as the world economy is fragmented and states feel threatened by others' militarization.

There may be some truth to this story, but it implies greater uniformity of thought and action among decisionmakers than can usually be found. Those who govern states may respond in many ways to economic privation, with only some of those responses culminating in external conflict, just as many kinds of noneconomic influences will affect the existence and timing of acts in the international arena. Sometimes a government will embody a great deal of goodwill and legitimacy in the eyes of its people. If so, economic hard times may be tolerated longer and with less defection from the governing party. (Note, for example, the tolerance shown for several years to the democratically elected government of Raúl Alfonsín in Argentina, which inherited an intractable economic mess from the unpopular military junta that preceded it.) Or an authoritarian government may have its populace so effectively cowed that protest may be suppressed, perhaps even without much overt government coercion of opponents.

A satisfactory explanation of war needs to take into account not just economics but political economy in the sense of characteristics of the government and the nature of its opposition. It is also possible that the degree of political opposition will have a complex effect. For example, assume that the government is widely regarded as legitimate, or that the economic downturn or recession is only a moderate one and does not occur near election time. If domestic discontent is slight, there may be no actions taken to affect the likelihood of conflict with foreigners. Pump-priming, if it exists, may be confined largely to cutting taxes and increasing civil spending, and there may be little hostility that requires diverting toward outsiders. More serious or prolonged economic difficulties may produce more desperate pump-priming (including military spending), and result in higher levels of popular discontent. Faced with such discontent, even a democratically elected government may feel some temptation to try to divert hostility toward foreign adversaries, and may be so preoccupied with its domestic problems that it exaggerates the hostility of foreign adversaries or wishfully exaggerates its chances of cowing or defeating them (Jervis, 1976).

Democratic governments may even be more tempted to do

this than authoritarian regimes accustomed to using force or threats to repress dissent. An authoritarian government may be able to handle even serious discontent by strengthening military and security forces and directing those forces solely against domestic opponents. For both democratic and authoritarian regimes, the incentives for international conflict may actually decrease when large-scale force is turned against domestic dissenters. With its hands and guns fully engaged in suppressing open rebellion or civil war, a government may want to avoid taking on a foreign adversary. If anything, it may become the target of a traditional enemy, as when the revolutionary but economically enfeebled government of Iran was attacked by Iraq in 1980. Thus attempts to divert hostility toward foreign adversaries may be most common with moderate rather than either very low or very high levels of economic distress, especially as that distress is translated into political opposition to the government. Moreover, and contrary to common assumptions, those motives may be more often found in democratic governments (which will be loath, or unable, to suppress dissent harshly and vigorously), or in authoritarian governments where the elites are already bitterly divided, than in relatively united authoritarian regimes. (Exception: those authoritarian regimes with innately aggressive or jingoistic ideologies.)

Yet another complication in finding a clear association between the state of the economy (and implicitly, consequent degrees of political opposition to or satisfaction with the government) and actions in the international arena lies in the timing of those actions. International conflicts are not likely to follow immediately on the heels of an economic downturn, especially if the relationship runs through an intermediary process of domestic militarization and international threat-perception. It takes time for a downturn to be recognized as such by political authorities, and more time for its impact to be felt in the political consciousness of the populace. If the authorities decide to try to cushion the impact by pump-priming in the military sector, plans must be drawn up and funds appropriated and spent. It takes time to build and design the weapons that military commanders will require, and it takes time to train the troops that are to use them. Military bureaucracies must prepare and obtain some consensus on war plans. The populace in general must be prepared, with clear images of who their enemies are and of the cause that may justify war against them. In short, preparations for war or military confrontation take time, perhaps one year or several. Meanwhile, a period of talking tough and making fairly mild threats toward a foreign adversary may ensue, both as a diversion from the continuing economic troubles and as possible preparation for more severe military confrontations to come.

If the process of preparation does take several years, the lag from economic downturn to conflict may well be so long that the conflict may occur only when the economy has already begun to recover. This will especially be the case if a pump-priming exercise of militarization is successful. If militarization produces a kind of prosperity, as intended, of course the conflict will occur during a period of (perhaps recent and relative) prosperity.

Consider the most destructive war of all time. Surely Adolf Hitler could not have come to power without the terrible economic depression that swept Germany at the beginning of the 1930s. Hitler certainly was bent on external adventures and aggression from the start, but it took time to tighten his grip on the German polity, to create an efficient propaganda division, to test his enemies' resolve, and, most importantly, to build the powerful military machine that might promise success in war. Thus Hitler ascended to power in 1933 but did not seriously risk war until 1936 or 1938. His preparations extended years after the depth of the depression, and indeed were crucial in ending that depression. But the subsequent prosperity should not disguise the fact that he was allowed to set out on his course by popular despair over economic hardships.

Electoral Politics and Economic Decline

In a democracy the state of the economy is a major determinant of electoral success. Inflation and unemployment are both unpopular; in the past they tended usually to be alternatives, with an analytical principle called the Phillips curve suggesting that a decrease in one could be obtained only at the expense of an increase in the other. More recently, especially in economies vulnerable to swings in the terms of foreign trade, they have frequently occurred together. Jimmy Carter was hit by both, as observers applied the term "misery index" (previously referring to the weather: temperature plus relative humidity) to the economy as the combination of the unemployment rate and the interest rate. The same problem, from the Arab oil embargo, had previously magnified the damage of Watergate to Republican candidates in the 1974 congressional election.

The impact of prosperity or unemployment is always distributed unevenly in a population, so that there will be some gainers even in a recession. Inflation might not be perceived as a political problem if all citizens' incomes and expenses were going up at the same time—but of course they don't. In runaway inflation the real problem is the impoverishment of those on fixed incomes (nonunionized workers, holders of fixed-rate loans or pensions) while others (unionized workers with cost-of-living contracts, debtors or creditors with adjustable rate loans) keep steady real incomes and still others (debtors with fixed rate loans) are enriched. It may be useful, therefore, to analyze separately the political effects of recession and inflation. But for a basic understanding of the political effects of economic conditions in modern democracies where very high inflation is rare, the two can be combined. And it is a matter of the recent rate of change ("what have you done for me lately?") rather than some absolute state of the economy. Voters' memories are short enough for them to look favorably on a government that has presided over a recent economic recovery even if the recovery followed a recession induced not long before by that same government. (Recall Reagan's popularity in the 1984 campaign despite the recession of 1981–82.)

The best single predictor of the governing party's electoral fortunes is the direction and rate of change in real (that is, inflation-adjusted) disposable income during the nine or twelve months preceding the election, perhaps mostly only the last three months. Presidents are held more accountable than are congressional candidates. Moderate inflation can be tolerated so long as average money incomes are going up faster than inflation. But a decline, or even only a very small improvement, in real income spells trouble. Worse yet for the politicians, hard times usually have more electoral impact than do good ones. People whose economic conditions have declined are more likely to blame the government and society at large for their plight than those whose conditions have improved are likely to credit the government or society. In the individualistic self-perception, I can make it by myself; if I don't, others are to blame.[2]

Voters of course react both to changes in their own conditions and to what they perceive as happening in the economy at large. They are not merely self-interested pocketbook voters; they react also with a sense of public-spiritedness and view of what is good for wider groups or for the national interest. Some analysts even conclude that "citizens seem to pay principal attention to the nation's economic predicament, and comparatively little to their own" (Kinder, 1981, p. 17; also Russett and Hanson, 1975; Kelman, 1987, ch. 11; and esp. Kinder, Adams, and Gronke, 1989). In this people respond strongly to information and images in the mass media—especially television, where scenes of unemployment lines can make a powerful impact even on people who are not directly affected. As the focus is removed from immediate personal experience, many issues become subject to "symbolic" politics (Iyengar and Kinder, 1987).

Knowing voters' sensitivity to the state of the business cycle, governments in turn try to manipulate the economy so as to produce the necessary popular support. "No president can have an economic policy; all his policies must be political. Economic policies are only the means to the end of maintaining the president's power and prestige" (Rose, 1985, p. 269, citing Richard Neustadt). Leaders will try to stimulate the economy shortly before elections, with some combination of tax cuts, spending increases, and acceleration of government payments that might not otherwise occur until after election day. Tax increases, spending cuts, and recessions are best postponed until after election day. The business cycle affects elections, and in turn the electoral cycle produces a policy cycle of vote-oriented action. Military spending may be an especially attractive candidate for election-oriented timing, since the amounts are large, since such spending often attracts support from conservatives who would not approve of additional spending for civilian purposes, and

2. The classic study is Kramer, 1971. Scores of works have subsequently elaborated the point, for the United States, Western Europe, Israel, and other countries. See, for example, Nordhaus, 1975; Tufte, 1978; Kiewiet, 1983; MacKuen, 1983; Ben Hanen and Temkin, 1986; Lewis-Beck, 1985; and Hibbs, 1987; a good review on the United States is Simonton, 1987. Monroe, 1984, suggests some caveats. On the blame and credit due to government see Bloom and Price, 1975; Abramowitz et al., 1988.

since acquisitions of equipment can in some degree be hastened or delayed without much obvious effect on security in peacetime.

Economic conditions, however, often cannot be controlled sufficiently to insure electoral success. Fine-tuning of a complex modern economy is less than an exact science. Timing is difficult. Some policy actions, such as cutting interest rates, may work relatively quickly, but in the United States monetary policy is basically made by the Federal Reserve Bank, and seems not to be usually affected by electoral considerations (Beck, 1984). Major increases in expenditure or cuts in taxes typically require months or even years to put into effect. Stimulation of the domestic economy may be impossible without unacceptable impacts on the balance of payments. Government interventions will help some people but are likely to hurt others (for example, through creating shortages and inflation in particular sectors). Even if the chief executive knows what he wants to do, the legislature may have other ideas. An American president is in a special pickle with an independent Congress, which often does not even have a majority of his party. As Allen Schick, a leading scholar of the budgetary process, put it, the president "makes the budget, but that doesn't mean he controls it" (quoted in Rose, 1988, p. 199).

Decisions to expand or reduce military spending of course will respond chiefly to changes in the international environment, although military expenditure also may manipulated partly to boost the economy around election times. Allocations for military manpower may be especially susceptible to election management; purchases of equipment, subject to long lead-times and production bottlenecks, may be less manipulable. U.S. military procurement contracts have tended to rise in the months immediately preceding elections, but the actual increases in expenditure are not enough to have much macroeconomic impact. That, and the fact that the increases are typically larger in years of congressional than presidential elections, suggests that the political motivation is less to stimulate the economy in general than to give friendly representatives and senators something for which to claim political credit with their constituents.[3]

---

3. The existence of a policy cycle in the United States was first demonstrated by Tufte, 1978. Important qualifications have been noted by Brown and Stein, 1982;

The business cycle thus is substantially less controllable than the policy cycle, and less predictable than the electoral cycle. Before John Maynard Keynes, of course, knowledge of how to control the business cycle was even less satisfactory. In the early 1930s, for instance, governments of the industrial democracies—Britain, France, and the United States—did just the wrong thing, cutting public spending (especially that for military purposes) and trying to achieve balanced budgets in the teeth of the depression. Germany, Italy, and Japan did just the opposite.

Even if the economy could be reliably heated up on command, that would not be enough. Political pressures are greatest at election time: the leader's election can never be certain enough, the victory margin never large enough. A legislator hopes primarily just to be elected; a presidential candidate must be concerned with his margin, and the hope that his coattails may be long enough to pull in his party's legislative candidates. In Samuel Kernell's words (1986, p. 188), "As election nears, a president will be tempted to husband even what he regards as surplus support. Accordingly, an unpopular president nearing election should come as close to resembling a single-minded popularity maximizer as one will find."

Yet the president (or prime minister) needs political support all the time. In a real sense he is in a never-ending electoral campaign. Theodore Lowi (1985) talks about "the plebiscitary presidency," in which the chief executive is constantly under pressure to solve problems. Many problems cannot be "solved" even with the resources of the chief executive of the world's most powerful state, but the president must at least give the appearance of solving them. These pressures apply at all times during an executive's tenure in office. Popularity with the voters

---

Alt and Chrystal, 1983; and Thompson and Zuk, 1983. Suggestions of manipulation of United States military spending to improve prospects in elections were found by Nincic and Cusack, 1979, contested by Krell, 1981, and identified again by Mintz and Hicks, 1984; Mintz, 1988a, for military manpower but not weapons procurement or research and development. Mintz, 1988b, and Mintz and Ward, 1988, 1989, also found a policy cycle for military spending in Israel, especially for manpower compensation climbing in election years. The definitive work on the electoral politics of military spending in the United States will be Mayer, 1991. In parliamentary systems, of course, the leader has the option of calling the election at a time when the economy is already prosperous, rather than having to try to induce prosperity for a fixed election time.

is a leader's most important resource for accomplishing any of his goals; a leader who allows that popularity to atrophy will quickly find his legislative program a casualty. In the words of a congressional staffer, "When you go up to the Hill and the latest polls show Carter isn't doing well, then there isn't much reason for a member to go along with him" (quoted in Jacobson, 1983, pp. 179–180).

A president operates within the triangle of forces and must persuade officials and legislators to follow him. The president "must gain and maintain the *reputation* for power, in hopes that the reputation for power will produce power itself"; he "must somehow mobilize the electorate in order to mobilize the elite" (Lowi, 1985, pp. 139, 165). If he can persuade others that the public is on his side (whether or not it "really" is) he wins. Support for the president in the polls is fairly highly correlated over time with support for the president in Congress, especially on foreign policy (Edwards, 1980, ch. 4). Popularity ratings are coin of the realm in legislative-executive wheedling and dealing. "Presidential approval ratings have created a pseudo-parliamentary situation, whereby the president faces a monthly vote of confidence . . . Incumbent administrations come to feel that they have no choice but to behave as if they are always in the midst of an election campaign" (Crespi, 1980, p. 42).

The direct appeal for public support as a means to twist arms in the Washington establishment is not risk-free. Every member of that establishment rules a semi-independent fiefdom; they do not like having their arms twisted, especially in public. The routine appeal to public opinion, even by the greatest communicator, "is more akin to force than to bargaining . . . it makes subsequent compromise with other politicians difficult" (Kernell, 1986, p. 4; also Neustadt, 1980). Woodrow Wilson fell afoul of this dilemma long ago. He waged his campaign for the League of Nations at two levels—one at the level of popular rhetoric to create the appearance or fact of support among the voters, and the other at the level of direct negotiations to persuade a two-thirds majority of the Senate to go along. But the excess of rhetoric with which he tried to rally the public was not consistent with the kind of nuanced discussions he needed to carry on with the senators (Tulis, 1987, pp. 147–161).

If a leader's foreign and domestic policy is mired in immobilism and he cannot control the economy enough to quiet the political opposition, then other instruments of political management must be found. Here is where the possibility of distracting attention or diverting anger can come in—and what better target than foreigners, who don't vote in one's elections and may not be much liked anyway?

These theories are part of a large corpus of social-psychological theories which assert that leaders of groups may often, and often successfully, try to divert the hostility derived from frustrations into aggressive words or acts toward outsiders (LeVine and Campbell, 1972, esp. ch. 8). Economic downturn, coming after a period of prosperity, growth, and rising expectations, can easily generate high levels of frustration for elites and public alike. If frustration leads to aggressive behavior at the mass level, the leaders of national societies may show similar tendencies both as they respond to popular moods and as they manipulate them when they see their own political fortunes endangered by the economic decline. Ned Lebow's studies (1981, 1985) of failures of deterrence found numerous cases in which the motivation for an aggressive foreign policy derived from the weakness of a state's political system, or the weakness of particular leaders in an intra-elite power struggle.

When the second oil shock of 1979 hit the economy only a year before Jimmy Carter was to run for reelection, his chief domestic adviser, Stuart Eizenstat, urged that all the blame be laid on foreigners: "With strong steps we can mobilize the nation around a real crisis and with a clear enemy—OPEC." Carter heeded the advice, and in his nationwide address declared, "Our neck is stretched over the fence and OPEC has the knife" (Epstein, 1983, p. 73). For leaders of more vulnerable states, however, this is a risky strategy. Heinrich Bruning, chancellor of the German Weimar Republic, tried making speeches directed toward Western public opinion on his commitment to peace and international cooperation so as to obtain agreement to scaling down the war reparations and permitting some German rearmament. Almost in the same breath he was trying to outflank nationalism by promising to be unyielding in obtaining redress of German grievances. He was not notably successful in either effort (Craig and George, 1983, p. 70).

Diversionary or scapegoating theories of war have a long history, with many examples that seem plausible. Verbal bashing of foreigners may become the policy of choice, and may very possibly lead to serious disputes and even war. An example where war was probably not expected but certainly risked, and experienced, is the Falklands/Malvinas conflict between Argentina and Britain in 1982. The Argentine junta was faced with continuing economic difficulty and political unrest—despite, and because of, repression. People were tired of a regime that had engaged in the "dirty war" against its own people and simultaneously bungled the economy (as many previous Argentine governments had bungled it). The Argentine government had a long-standing claim to the Malvinas Islands, a claim that seemed to be making no progress in negotiations with Britain. Seizure of the islands could both satisfy an old aspiration and serve at least immediately to rally nationalist political support behind the regime. The British failed to give any convincing signals that they would defend the islands, and the Argentine military leaders persuaded themselves that the United States would not interfere. If the seizure of the islands had succeeded, against little or no British resistance, it would have left the regime greatly strengthened in popularity. So Argentina's economic troubles helped impel the government to choose that particular moment for military action.

Unfortunately for the Argentines, the British did resist vigorously. On its side of the Atlantic, Margaret Thatcher's government was in the midst of Britain's most severe post–World War II economic troubles, with very high unemployment, continuing inflation, and stagnation of production. The Conservatives were unpopular, trailing badly in the public opinion polls. It was not the time for making "generous" concessions to a foreign power; the government could not afford to appear irresolute. It fought back, and won. The victory helped sustain Thatcher's popularity into a successful election campaign a year later (Norpoth, 1987; however, Sanders et al., 1987, doubt that the boost in popularity lasted a year).

Despite the number of plausible examples from personal or national experience which almost everyone can cite, evidence for a generally operating causal connection between conflict at home and conflict abroad is somewhat ambiguous (Stohl, 1980; Zinnes 1980). The reason for lack of systematic evidence, however, may be less in the absence of some such connection than in the lack of clear theoretical specification of the circumstances—when and how, and by whom—in which international scapegoating is likely to occur (Levy, 1989).

Rallying 'round the Flag

Except in a protracted war, much foreign policy is literally and figuratively distant from most citizens; its interpretation is thus particularly subject to selective release of information and careful media presentation—a prime candidate for symbolic politics. It is also the area in which the chief of state typically operates with the least immediate legislative constraint. "External constraints and conventional purposes have largely closed off the domestic scene as a field of great action. It is in foreign policy— with its inherent drama, its freedom of action, its momentous consequences—that presidential heroes are made." (Miroff, 1976, p. 281).

There is some hyperbole in this quotation, yet one kind of foreign policy action—a short, low-cost military measure to repel an attack—is almost invariably popular at least at its inception. So too are many other kinds of assertive action or speech in foreign policy. This is true for both authoritarian regimes and democracies. First demonstrated for Presidents Roosevelt and Truman after Pearl Harbor and the American defense of South Korea in 1950, the phenomenon has come to be known as the "rally 'round the flag effect" (Smith, 1971; Mueller, 1973; refined by Kernell, 1978, and Brody, 1984).[4] It seems to apply to Congress as well as to the public; for example, the president is more likely to win congressional approval on key international issues in the month following the international use of military force (Stoll, 1987).

According to the initial formulation of the rally 'round the flag phenomenon, almost anything that happened in foreign affairs—whether a "tough" action by the president like using or

4. In militarily weak states the effect can be dramatic even in the event of major policy conflict with allies. For example, support for a ban on nuclear weapons entering New Zealand nearly doubled (from 40 to 76 percent) after the government adopted the ban and the United States followed with a confrontational policy. See LaMare, 1987.

threatening to use force, a "conciliatory" action like signing a treaty, or some shock from outside the United States, like the Iranian seizure of hostages or the Soviet success in putting the first satellite into space—has an immediately favorable effect on the president's popularity. This effect is short-term, typically not more than a month or two in duration, after which his popularity rating drops back to about where it was (or even below if, as in the case of the Iran hostage affair, the president is unable to cope with the situation). A very similar phenomenon can be seen in Israel, with big but very brief jumps in popular approval of the government's "handling of the general situation" during Israel's brief wars, the Entebbe hostage rescue, and Egyptian Premier Anwar Sadat's dramatic visit in 1977, and smaller jumps for other less dramatic confrontational or conciliatory international events (Stone, 1982, p. 217).

The common increase in popularity even for events that seem to hurt the country probably stems from the reluctance of political and media elites to criticize the president immediately. On national security matters there is always a substantial possibility that the president has access to secret information which he can selectively release so as to make a critic look foolish or even disloyal (Brody and Shapiro, 1987). The charge of disloyalty is always a greater risk when one criticizes a leader who takes forceful action against an adversary than when one charges that a leader has been too conciliatory, giving away the store. Given the lack of elite disapproval of forceful actions, majority approval of the Grenada invasion or the bombing of Libya is hardly surprising.[5] Thus the rally effect probably is strongest for tough actions.

John Kennedy's Cuban policy in the fall of 1962 illustrates the electoral pressures and rewards for an assertive if not rash foreign policy confrontation during the cold war era. Louis Harris was the president's pollster; Kennedy adviser and speechwriter Theodore Sorenson kept close track of the polls by Harris and others on Cuba, from the time of the Bay of Pigs fiasco. Sorenson

5. By contrast, when elite disapproval emerges in a prompt and widespread manner, popular disapproval may also be very great. Recall that following disclosure of the Iran-Contra affair (which political competitors could safely criticize as a deal with the terrorist adversary Iran) President Reagan's popularity dropped almost 20 percentage points in two weeks.

characterized Cuba as JFK's "Achilles heel." In a mid-September AIPO (Gallup) poll asking what should be done about Cuba, 10 percent advocated some form of military force—bombing, invading, or other belligerent acts—and another 13 percent some form of trade embargo; 26 percent favored doing "something short of war," and 22 percent keeping hands off. This was after the first public charge by Senator Kenneth Keating that the Soviets were putting offensive weapons in Cuba, but before his more detailed and alarming public accusation. In fact the president was considering "something short of war"—a renewed effort named operation Mongoose to overthrow Castro, to culminate at the electorally convenient time of October 1962. In the actual Cuban missile crisis something between an embargo and bombing or invading—the blockade—was Kennedy's choice of the least he could do in the light of either domestic political pressures or international exigencies. His job performance rating rose dramatically in one of only nine times since World War II that an increase of 10 percent or greater could be attributed to a foreign policy "rally" (Kern et al., 1983, pp. 100, 103–104, 256; Edwards, 1983, p. 244).

Dramatic political events that occur or continue during the intense period between Labor Day and the November election have a direct effect on the ability of the president's party to hold or gain seats in Congress. A study of eleven such events (mostly connected to foreign policy) and nineteen post–World War II elections found that the effect was greater when a significant fraction of the population had "no opinion" on whether the president was doing a good job. The seven dramatic events seen as positive in their effects typically were worth three seats in Congress for every 2 percent of the population that had no opinion in the popularity poll, and the four negative events (like the combination of Suez and Hungary in 1956, or the Iran hostages in 1980) similarly cost about that many seats. Since as much as 15 percent of the population sometimes had no opinion on the president's performance, the effect of these events on the partisan balance of power in Congress could be substantial (Marra and Ostrom, 1989).

The president's speeches can be a powerful political tool. His popularity ratings typically are raised 4 to 6 percentage points in the short term by a prime-time speech on foreign policy. A sharp and dramatic illustration of this comes from a Washington Post/ABC three-day poll which happened to straddle the night of President Reagan's speech on Lebanon of October 17, 1983. On the day before the speech 41 percent of the sample said they approved of his policy in Lebanon; on the following day the percentage was 52 (and within two months it had dropped back again; see Powlick, 1989). Tough talk or behavior toward the Soviet Union, or a major threat or use of force in Europe, the Middle East, or Central America, similarly raises the president's popularity ratings. The effects of other manipulable elements of political drama, such as foreign travel or diplomacy, are uncertain. In general, nine voters in ten approve of "frequent summit meetings . . . even if no new arms control agreements have been signed," but some instances of cooperation with the Soviet Union have been followed by drops of 1 or 2 percent in the president's approval ratings (Ostrom and Simon, 1985; Americans Talk Security, July 1988, p. 33; Marra, Ostrom, and Simon, 1989).

The matter of a drop in popularity from seeming too favorable toward the Soviet Union is not quite so simple as these findings suggest. It depends very much on the context of the action and what kind of president is taking it; Ronald Reagan's last two years in office suggest some qualifications. We will consider the matter again in the next chapter. What is clear is that seeming tough rarely hurts much, at least in the short run. Given the benefit of the doubt often accorded to a president when acting in the arcane arena of foreign affairs, manipulation of foreign crises for domestic political purposes may be less visible than similar manipulation of macroeconomic policy.

Support for the use of military force against foreign adversaries is nearly always lower in the abstract than in concrete situations. When asked in opinion surveys about hypothetical occasions to use force, most people disapprove. But their immediate reaction to an actual use of military force is almost invariably favorable, as it has been in instances including Lebanon, the Dominican Republic, the *beginnings* of the Vietnam war, and the Mayaguez affair, as well as the invasion of Grenada and the bombing of Libya. For instance, before President Johnson sent U.S. troops to Vietnam following the Tonkin Gulf incident, only 42 percent of the populace said they supported involvement in Vietnam;

shortly afterward, 72 percent did so. Similarly, before it happened only 7 percent endorsed the idea of invading Cambodia; after Nixon did it 50 percent approved (Weissberg, 1976, p. 235, cited in Nincic, 1988b, p. 72; Benson, 1982).

Invoking the Rally

How does the rally effect operate in the context of elections and economic distress? According to one study (Stoll, 1984), post–World War II American presidents were more likely to use military force if they were seeking reelection during a developing or ongoing war; that is, when a president knew that voters would be more concerned than usual with foreign affairs, and thus more likely to hold it against him if the war went badly. This analysis is limited by the fact that in most years the United States has been at peace, so the wartime election years (Korea and Vietnam) provide a very small sample from which to generalize. But psychologists have established that American presidents' foreign policy rhetoric toward the Soviet Union becomes more simplistic (its cognitive complexity declines) in the latter half of election years (Suedfeld and Tetlock, 1977; Tetlock, 1985), and that a decline in cognitive complexity by leaders is in turn associated with a greater likelihood of undertaking military interventions and a decreasing likelihood of arriving at international agreements (Tetlock and McGuire, 1985).

Another and more complex study of the same time period showed that presidents were more likely to use force when the economy was experiencing inflation or high unemployment (either element of the misery index) and the percentage of the population considering the economy to be the "most important problem" was high. The authors also found, though less certainly, a tendency for the use of force to be more common in the months immediately preceding an election. A president was especially likely to use force if his popularity rating was in the "critical" 40-to-60-percent range rather than very high or very low—in other words, when he most needed the boost in popularity (Ostrom and Job, 1986).

A recent decline in popularity strengthens this temptation. Relevant examples include Lyndon Johnson's authorization of the bombing of Hanoi in 1966 and Jimmy Carter's go-ahead to the attempt to rescue the hostages in Iran in 1980. At high levels of public support the president has little need for a further boost; at low levels—when he is wounded politically, with his blood in the water—military action may call forth criticism from opponents emboldened by his vulnerability (Ostrom and Simon, 1985). Presidential use of military force is more likely when the recent decline in approval is greater within supporters of his own party than among the opposition (whom he may discount anyway). It also happens faster when the president's approval rating among his partisans starts below 50 percent than if it is initially very high (Morgan and Bickers, 1989).

To be sure, these illustrations and statistical findings tell only part of the story. A national leader has only a limited amount of choice about whether and when to use military force. If an adversary acts aggressively against what is considered an important national interest, the state of the domestic political economy may be only marginally relevant to decisions about how to respond. The above analyses apply only to the post–World War II era, for which the public opinion data are adequate. That era, however, does coincide with the period in which American presidents, as leaders of a global superpower, have acquired the ability as commander-in-chief to use military force quickly and without consultation. But the politically relevant timing of international events is not just a recent phenomenon. The most substantial evidence for economic and electoral incentives to use force stems from my own examination of the actions of American presidents during a much longer span of time—the past century (Russett, 1990). Over this period, presidents were more likely to use or threaten to use military force in years when the economy had been doing badly, or, if the economy was doing well, when there was a national election.[6] American involvement in new military disputes was least likely when the economy had been expanding nicely and there was no election (see Table 2.1). Militarized disputes also were somewhat more

6. As noted below, the same finding about the state of the economy applied to Great Britain. But there was no relation between military conflict and British elections—not surprisingly, since the British prime minister has substantial freedom to call elections at a favorable time, and so is under less pressure to create a good political climate for a fixed election time.

Table 2.1. U.S. involvement in new militarized international disputes, 1873–1988, according to whether there was an election in that year and the state of the economy.

	GDP per capita increase below 1% two years previously		GDP per capita increase above 1% two years previously	
	Election	No election	Election	No election
% of years with new militarized dispute	75	74	73	41
No. of years	16	19	22	21

Source: Russett, 1990, updated here. Many years in the period are excluded because the United States was already, from the previous year, engaged in a high-level militarized dispute.

likely when the election was for president rather than just an off-year congressional campaign.

Jimmy Carter offers a fairly recent example that nicely fits the pattern. In April 1980 the economy was in the condition of high inflation and recession. Carter's popularity was low, and a presidential election loomed; more acutely, he was facing a vigorous and immediate primary challenge, from Edward Kennedy, for renomination. He decided, against the advice of his secretary of state, Cyrus Vance, to attempt the high-risk military operation to rescue the hostages in Iran. The rescue failed, but for a while Carter was rewarded in the polls and at the polls. Doubtless his motives were more complex than simply calculations of his own political interest. But we may reasonably suspect that such motives played a part, even though they are not the sort of thing which is likely to emerge prominently in the memoirs.

In the statistical analysis, the association with election times was much stronger in the years from the 1870s to 1930 than later, and the association with economic downturn was much stronger in the post-1930 period. Presidents have been held more accountable for hard times since the creation of modern economic theories and instruments for the control of the economy. At the same time, the polls and the electronic media have created a kind of permanent referendum on the president, compelling him to produce constant evidence of his popularity regardless of the timing of elections. Another study of American politics over this century-long period also found a mild association of low-level uses of military force with recession, but found that full-scale wars were more likely to occur at times of prosperity. This may be because a decision to go to war requires a high level of popular consensus—more easily reached in prosperous times—but low-level and less consequential uses of force may be more common in efforts to *achieve* a consensus that had previously been elusive (Elder and Holmes, 1988).

Results like these fit well with a perspective on a rational president trying to maximize the chances that he or his party will retain the presidency, and secondarily to maximize the number of his supporters in Congress. (Presumably a president would care more about his own reelection, or bringing in his successor, than about trying to affect a congressional election in which presidential coattails are usually not very long anyway.) Although the data base for this analysis remains fairly small (fewer than eighty years for observations) the evidence is at least as strong as that for successful presidential manipulation of the economy in accord with the electoral cycle. "The desperate search is no longer for the good life but for the most effective presentation of appearances. This is a pathology because it escalates the rhetoric at home, ratcheting expectations upward notch by notch, and fuels adventurism abroad" (Lowi, 1985, p. 20).

Moreover, if toughness is more likely than conciliation to glean electoral rewards, a president who is aware of this can be expected to tailor his foreign policy accordingly. Apparently most are, and do. Spending on strategic weapons tends to be highest in presidential election years and also high, from carryovers, in the immediately subsequent year. Such spending tends to be lowest in the third year of a president's term. Arms control agreements typically show just the opposite pattern: they are most common in the president's third year and least so in the first and fourth. Also, in the only two second elected terms we have seen since World War II—those of Eisenhower and Reagan—policy has generally been more conciliatory than in the first, when the president had to be concerned about his prospects for reelection (Nincic, 1990; also Cusack, 1989).

It is important to extend our view beyond the United States (and, more so, beyond just superpower relations in the nuclear era). Another analysis looked at limited uses of force (not full-scale war) by the Israeli government. During most of its history Israel has been subjected to various raids, shellings, and terrorist attacks from beyond its borders, and in response has pursued policies of reprisal and occasionally preemptive strikes. The external attacks were real enough, but often presented a fair degree of choice as to whether, and when, Israel should strike. Controlling for the timing of Arab military operations, the Israeli government was more likely to use military force in election years than at other times. Moreover, during election years Israeli military operations were more common in the months before the election than after it. A high level of Arab military action alone was a virtually necessary but not a sufficient condition for a high level of Israeli military action, but if the Arab operations happened before an election Israeli military actions were almost certain (Barzilai and Russett, 1990). This pattern closely resembles that for the United States, despite the special intensity of security concerns in Israel and the mythology that security matters there are kept autonomous from partisan politics.

Possibly the Israeli government felt under greater public pressure, as election time drew near, to yield to a continually hawkish public mood and to do something about the Arab attacks. That explanation, however, seems dubious given the general observation that concrete military actions are more popular immediately after they are taken than when they were merely hypothetical. More likely, the government was deliberately attempting to rally greater support. A more psychological and less politically cynical interpretation is that government leaders suffer from a not fully conscious form of misperception, exaggerating the degree and importance of external hostility at times when they themselves are most insecure politically—at election times—and hence react more vigorously at those times than otherwise.

A vivid example of the conjuncture of security policy and electoral politics is Israel's raid on the Iraqi nuclear reactor at Osirak on June 7, 1981, just three weeks before Prime Minister Menachem Begin was to face the voters in a general election. There was substantial military justification for the strike—the reactor might have begun to operate a few months later—and the Iran-Iraq war made the international situation favorable for

Israel. Yet almost certainly the strike could have been postponed until after the election without harm to Israeli security. As it was, Begin's party benefited greatly from an outpouring of popular approval despite severe economic difficulties (from inflation rather than recession). The action, especially its timing, was the subject of much partisan comment (Sachar, 1987, pp. 127–131).

Again, specific examples must be put into the context of results from larger comparative analyses, in this case statistical studies of many countries over long time periods. These studies lose much of the fine-grained detail one would like to have about timing, circumstances, and decisionmakers' conscious calculations of advantage and motivation. But their virtue lies in illuminating some broad patterns. One such study over a century-long period (Russett, 1990) found that democratic states (but not authoritarian ones) were more likely to engage in international disputes, involving the threat or use of military force, in years after their gross national product had declined. The fact that this happened often only in democratic countries is consistent with the thesis that leaders of democracies are held more immediately and directly accountable for economic conditions than are autocratic leaders.

Closer analysis showed that the pattern was substantially confined to the United States and Great Britain—great powers which have had much more control than small states over if and when they will engage in international conflict. This association for the United States and Britain—powerful states that could be successfully attacked by few if any others—argues against the possibility that countries are more likely to become the victim, rather than the perpetrator, of aggressive acts when their economies are weak or their political systems are in some disarray. Also, the aggregated analyses did control for the initiator of the conflict (defined somewhat arbitrarily as the first party to use military force), and found that it made no difference.

By contrast with the democracies, authoritarian states showed some tendency to engage in foreign conflict when their economies were in an upswing, providing a surge of resources available for the war machine. This may reflect the different political dynamics of authoritarian regimes. Their leaders can use the repressive apparatus of the state to control dissent while they build up their military capability and use the buildup to bring about greater prosperity in the process, whereas democratic leaders are under more immediate, short-term pressures to satisfy popular discontent. But even in authoritarian states, leaders' perceptions of their own public matter; in 1914, for instance, the government of imperial Germany saw public opinion as an active, constraining, coercive force (Fagen, 1960). The emergence of sharp conflicts within a regime may create incentives analogous to the imminence of elections in democracies (Levy and Vakili, 1989).

Another cross-national analysis in the same study, limited to the period after 1953 but adding several measures of domestic political conflict, found that economic downturn did not significantly increase the likelihood that democracies would be involved in international disputes (Russett, 1990). But domestic political protest was strongly associated with such involvement. This was especially true if the government had previously tried to repress the protests, by arresting the protestors, forbidding demonstrations and strikes, or imposing censorship. Democracies are not very good at vigorously and overtly repressing dissidents—if they are good at this, they lose much of their democratic character. When they cannot repress internal protest effectively, they become more likely to engage in international conflicts. Thus economic downturns in themselves may do less to produce incentives toward international conflict than does domestic political conflict, from whatever cause.

In undemocratically governed countries the pattern was not too different. As with democracies, protest and rebellion at home were often followed by conflicts abroad. And whereas economic downturns did not play a direct role in these countries either, they worked indirectly by helping stimulate rebellions, which in turn often led to foreign conflicts. Thus there are several routes, appropriate to different kinds of political systems, whereby "rational" political leaders may seek to divert attention from many kinds of domestic troubles by discovering or engaging foreign enemies.

Crisis, War, and the Voters

This discussion should not be interpreted as meaning that democracies are necessarily more likely to engage in either war or lesser forms of international conflict than are states which are not democracies. They are not. The consensus of systematic studies is that type of political system is not related in general to the probability that a country will be involved in war or international conflict in general (Wallensteen, 1973; Small and Singer, 1976; Chan, 1984; Weede, 1984; Doyle, 1986; Gantzel, 1987; Domke, 1988, ch. 5; Maoz and Abdolali, 1989).[7] We have only been discussing the timing of conflicts, a matter which is partly under the control of a government. Regardless of timing, the United States has been more conflict-prone than most governments, but not more so than other great powers such as Britain and France and the Soviet Union. Great powers have wider interests, many more states which they can expect to defeat militarily, and greater capabilities for distant military engagements than do small powers, so they are more conflict-prone. There is also the fact that leaders of states, like ordinary people, learn. If they have succeeded, either internationally or in domestic politics, by using force, they are likely to continue using it (Gurr, 1988). These characteristics are distinct from anything peculiar to the United States, or to democracies in general.

Remember also that the results connecting economic downturn to international conflict apply only to engaging in relatively low-level international disputes and uses of military force, not to the large-scale exercise of international violence known as war (defined as producing more than a thousand fatalities). Real wars are both serious and rare. They are rare enough that we should not expect to find—and do not often find—any convincing regularities between economic or political cycles and the initiation of war in the modern era. Most examples are countered by contrary examples. That is not surprising, just because war is serious. Whereas the initiation of low-level international conflict may be influenced by considerations of domestic politics, the dynamics of escalation from confrontation into crisis into war typically are driven much more by the international environment and the behavior of one's adversary (Leng, 1984; Huth

---

7. Rummel, 1983, 1985, is the only dissenter, principally on the basis of a study of 1976–1980, a period that omits, among others, the Vietnam War and most postcolonial wars.

and Russett, 1988).[8] It is one thing to be willing to threaten or bash the foreigners verbally, or even to beat up on a few relatively weak foreigners. It is quite another to make a decision for war, or a decision that may lead one's adversary to decide for war.

Indeed, the assertion that carrying on a low-level quarrel with a foreign adversary by means of threats or small-scale uses of military force may be politically popular is not the same as asserting that *war* is popular. War—costly, often protracted, usually dangerous—is very different from a quick demonstrative or coercive use of military force. World War I, Korea, and Vietnam (though not World War II) are all regarded by the public as mistakes (Erskine, 1970; Smith, 1971).[9] Perhaps after a brief spurt of national unity, wars usually produce a loss of social cohesion and popular morale, manifested in higher rates of strikes, crime, and violent political protest (Stohl, 1975; Stein, 1980). Governments lose popularity in proportion to the war's cost in blood and money. Of the two, blood (American) seems the more important. In a survey offering ten criteria by which the use of American military forces abroad should be judged, the number of American lives that might be lost rated first, and the cost in dollars last (Americans Talk Security, October 1988).

Israeli backing for the war in Lebanon shows how drastically and rapidly popular support can be withdrawn from an unsuccessful war. Initially, in the summer of 1982, two-thirds of the

8. James, 1987, 1988, however, did find that governments were more likely to escalate military disputes when the dispute coincided with both an increase in domestic turmoil and an opportunity for a successful use of international force. He notes appropriately that war can offer an excuse to enhance centralized control of the domestic economy and polity. Tilly, 1985, likens the state to a protection racket, in that the plausibility of the state's claim to uniqueness in the legitimate exercise of violence depends on the existence of "illegitimate" competitors, internal or external.

9. Since this chapter and especially the next two make extensive use of survey research materials, a methodological note is required. It has long been understood that the answers obtained to survey questions depend importantly on cultural context, and also on how the questions are asked: how they are worded, and—less well appreciated—the order in which they are asked. Indeed, there often is no truly "neutral" question. See Hyman, 1972; Robinson and Meadow, 1982. The most valid and reliable use of survey data is for comparing different populations, within and between countries and over time. Where I refer to responses for one particular time and group I have tried to use several questions to tap the range of attitudes for a concept. I use the terms "opinion" and "attitude" interchangeably, as approved by McGuire, 1969.

population supported it. Three years later that support was down to 15 percent, and the greatest dropoff had occurred in the first ten months—by May 1983. Support was especially tenuous because the government failed to achieve its aims in the war, and because the public viewed this as more nearly a "war of choice" than one forced on Israel, as the 1973 and even 1967 wars had been (Arian, 1985).

Presidents Truman, Johnson, and Nixon all saw their popularity damaged by war. In congressional and presidential elections over nearly a century, in every case candidates of the party initiating a war did less well both during and immediately after the war than would have been predicted by the models that predict election results from the state of the economy. The longer and more costly the war, the greater the loss of votes. Even Franklin Roosevelt, with the "best" of wars, found his electoral margin in 1944 markedly below what it had been in 1940, and the Democrats suffered stunning losses in the congressional election of 1946 (Cotton, 1986).

Fears of the domestic political consequences of becoming involved in a real war work to restrain the belligerent actions of leaders. In hypothetical questions, actions to avert losses from Soviet invasion of friends or allies are more acceptable than are efforts to achieve gains, as by rolling back a previous Soviet acquisition. Actions against small adversaries are usually more popular than ones against the Soviet Union. In their implicit cost-benefit calculations, Americans seem not to put a high value on improvements in the international position of the United States as compared with substantial monetary costs, the loss of American lives, or the risk of expansion to a wider and more costly war.[10] Grenada was an appropriate target for American action precisely because its own military forces were so inconsequential, and Fidel Castro had already signaled that he was not prepared to intervene on behalf of Grenada's leaders. The risk of becoming bogged down in an extended military action was nil (unlike the possibility with Nicaragua). Similarly,

10. These calculations are entirely consistent with models of rational economic and psychological behavior, for instance as developed by Kahneman and Tversky, 1979. Elites are also cautious. According to Etheredge, 1978, p. 42, "men who enjoy competition are inclined to assert dominance in small countries but to hold this predisposition in check when faced with a direct confrontation by the Soviet Union."

in deciding to punish Libya's Gaddafi for terrorism, the American administration chose, with a clear eye toward public opinion, an air strike rather than a landing that might incur significant American casualties.

Faced with this mix of popular preferences, economic sanctions can provide a valuable instrument for government action. Sanctions—as against Cuba, the Soviet Union, or South Africa—offer an opportunity to express disapproval and impose costs (sometimes very limited ones) on an adversary while incurring virtually no risk of escalation to direct U.S. involvement. Thus despite evidence that economic sanctions rarely succeed in achieving their ostensible international goals, governments continue to employ them. They are seemingly successful in satisfying a popular demand to "do something" (Lindsay, 1986).

Other and smaller countries, near to great powers, must be still more circumspect. The Swedish government is careful not to antagonize its Soviet neighbor, whatever the vicissitudes of Sweden's economy. A bit of scapegoating may take place toward more distant powers who in no way pose a military threat, however; for example, vigorous Swedish protests against American policy in Vietnam and Nicaragua (Goldman, Berglund, and Sjöstedt, 1986).

Least healthy for a leader is of course to lose a war. All great-power governments that have lost major wars in the past century have been overthrown from within if not by their external enemies (Stein and Russett, 1980). But even leaders who conduct and *win* costly wars are likely to be "punished" by their long-suffering electorates. Recall the fate of Winston Churchill and the Conservatives in 1945.

Herein lies the risk for a leader who is tempted to garner short-term support by initiating belligerent moves in foreign policy. A threat to use military force may lead to an international crisis; the crisis may get out of hand and lead to a serious military engagement; military engagements may escalate and become prolonged. Despite these risks, the temptation is there. Both Vietnam and the earlier Bay of Pigs fiasco have been called instances when leaders "were driven into policy failures . . . by the conflicting imperatives of acting wherever the Communist challenge was raised, but adhering to the constraints of peace and keeping the war at the lowest possible level. The result was policies of bold commitment but compromised means" (Destler et al., 1984).

New research on the entry of democracies into war (whether initiated by the democracy itself or by a nondemocratic adversary) over the past century and a half finds war to be most likely in the months or year immediately after an election (Gaubatz, 1989). This is consistent with the theory and empirical results summarized above: Democratic leaders know that full-scale war is unpopular, and therefore avoid it shortly before election times if they can. But they may also, before the election, engage in crowd-pleasing actions less violent but still belligerent, which escalate crises and make it harder to avoid war in the somewhat longer run.

We are left with some disturbing implications about the difficulties of conducting national security policy in a democracy. The timing of international disputes is related to domestic economic conditions, and to the election cycle. Even if these disputes do not get out of hand and become wars, the combination of electoral politics and economic distress (or perhaps domestic political troubles stemming from other causes) is a dangerous one for international relations. Such a combination constitutes grounds for concern that the interests of governing elites, rather than broader "national" interests, may drive national security policy in pernicious ways. Political elites have a clear interest in keeping themselves in power. They must conduct foreign policy with a sharp eye to its domestic political consequences, and they may confound their personal interests with the national interest—believing, for instance, that the national interest would be ill served by allowing the domestic opposition to take power.

These results also suggest serious concerns about the appropriate timing for leaders to attempt cooperative or peacemaking moves toward other states. Arms control treaties, for instance, may not be well received in times of economic adversity. By this principle, the timing for consideration of the SALT II agreement by the U.S. Senate was doubly unpropitious. President Carter finally withdrew the treaty from Senate consideration in early 1980, following the Soviet invasion of Afghanistan. Coincidentally, however, the American economy was in recession, which may not have been the most promising context for ratification of a treaty requiring trust and conciliation with the nation's leading adversary. Future leaders contemplating such agreements may wish to take into account the state of the domestic economy as they ponder the degree of popular support, and try to adjust their timing accordingly. But the opportunities afforded by the electoral cycle are brief, when we consider not just the popular response but the need for intensive attention to domestic problems, at the expense of foreign ones, at various points in the cycle. We reviewed those constraints in Chapter 1 (see Destler et al., 1984, p. 269; Quandt, 1986, ch. 1).

A president who tries to act decisively in foreign policy at times that are usually devoted to other matters may fall on his face, a fall made more likely by the inexperience of most presidents in foreign policy. Most American presidents gain office because they know a great deal about domestic politics, not because of their level of knowledge of the wider world. Jimmy Carter's clumsiness provides an example, with his far-ranging but ill-conceived arms control proposal to the Soviet Union right after his inauguration. John Kennedy, with somewhat greater previous exposure to international affairs, had the Bay of Pigs disaster as testimony to his inexperience.

Remember, too, that if an agreement is sought it takes two to make it. Leaders of the other side have their own set of domestic constraints and cycles of succession to leadership, whatever their form of government. Periods of economic downturn for the Soviet Union may, unlike the case in democracies, be the times when "peace" or coexistence is most attractive. For example, slow domestic growth led Leonid Brezhnev to seek Western technological assistance and reduction of the Soviet military burden in the early 1970s; success (only partially forthcoming) in those efforts promised to promote his domestic political authority (Volten, 1982). Many analysts of Mikhail Gorbachev's more recent and more vigorous initiatives toward the West suggest similar motivations.

For now, the most important point is just that foreign policy is, in substantial degree, domestic policy. What we have found extends previous work which established that arms "races," while partly a phenomenon of reacting to what the other side is building, are also in large part "autistic" processes, driven by bureaucratic pressures and domestic politics (Senghaas, 1972; Russett, 1983a; Ward, 1984). We found that the influence of domestic politics applies strongly even to the threat of—and use of—lethal violence against foreign powers. To understand that threats and uses of international violence are shaped in important ways by a leader's concern for his or her domestic power base is to begin the process of demystifying the reasons and rationalizations often offered for those actions.

3

Realism and Idealism

Liberal democracy almost guarantees some circulation of
leadership so that great power is usually fleeting and no
vested interest lasts forever. The constitutional restraints
have always reinforced this style . . . The total effect is
that policy does not change either rapidly or sharply
enough to hurt anyone very badly . . .

William H. Riker, *Liberalism against Populism*

A bitter debate has long raged between self-styled "realist"
observers of international relations and "idealists" (sometimes
called "transnationalists"). These contending perspectives are
similar, though not identical, to popular distinctions between
"hawks" and "doves," and between conservatives and liberals.[1]
Such distinctions are simplistic—and in the next chapter we
will dissect them into a more complex multidimensional pattern—but they represent a useful initial cut.

The Range of Acceptable Options

At first blush such polarities seem to represent irreconcilable
principles, fundamentally opposed views of human nature and
of the right way to order world affairs or political life in general.
Yet most people incorporate some aspects of each opposing view
rather than epitomize the extreme points on these spectra. This
is true both of academic theorists and of ordinary citizens. The
mix between the two views in any particular individual's head,
and in the collective body politic, determines the range of acceptable action open to political leaders. Leaders may try to expand
their freedom of action by persuading much of the public to shift
its mixture of acceptable policy in one direction or the other. A

1. Given the abundant evidence that women are on average significantly more
dovish than men (Smith, 1984; Shapiro and Mahajan, 1986; Martilla, 1989, makes
some qualifications) one can also add a related masculine-feminine distinction.

great leader will actually do that. But the leader's ability to shift opinion is rarely great. Rather, the maneuvering space is restricted chiefly to the range of actions already deemed acceptable. We shall see how that range has been defined—sometimes differently for different leaders—and how it has changed over time.

For the hard-headed realist, world politics is a struggle for power, a competition between independent nation-states wherein a state that fails to pursue its self-interest in a tough-minded manner thereby risks its security and even its sovereignty. Since there is no superior government to enforce peace, each state must look out for itself and maintain a favorable balance of power. The idealist, by contrast, insists that competition is not all, that even adversarial states must often cooperate in order to achieve their goals. Many interests are common rather than competing; states must cooperate to provide a basis for international trade and finance, and enemies usually have shared interests in avoiding wars and severe arms races.

On the hawk-dove spectrum, hawks emphasize competitive elements, the need to keep up one's military strength to deter war; also they are ready to use that strength periodically in order to defend their own sphere of interest and to reduce the adversary's. Their favorite historical analogy is Munich and the "appeasement" of 1938. Hawks talk about how "our" interests differ from "theirs," and of the need to maintain the separateness, the borders, between us and them. Doves reply with words about the need for cooperation to avoid war and the risks of provoking the adversary. They prefer negotiations for arms control and disarmament to reliance on unilateral action. Their favorite historical analogy is likely to be 1914, when arguably the major powers stumbled into a massively destructive war that none of them really wanted. Doves speak of connectedness, the need to find common ground and a community of interests transcending national borders.

Modern-day conservatives laud the possibilities of individual action, by persons and, internationally, by nations acting alone. Political liberals decry unfettered individualism as destroying natural bonds of community and mutual aid.

At their extremes, all these characterizations are caricatures. Each has a bit of the truth. States and individuals do compete and do cooperate. War is a risk; sometimes it arises from unrestrained aggression and sometimes from fear or desperation. Political leaders may start from one side or another of these spectra, but soon find that in the realities of world politics they must incorporate elements of both in their actions. They also soon discover that most of their constituents are not to be found at either end, and that to retain political support a leader must in some way combine the rhetoric as well as the reality of both sides. The successful mixture will vary over time and circumstance; more than one mixture may work for any given circumstance. Yet no leader can ignore the need to find a mix of "practical realism," tailored to perceptions of that leader's particular strengths and weaknesses.

Leaders may recognize that in many instances members of the public are willing to accept any of several alternative policies in pursuit of a general goal like "peace and security." One of the clearest examples is the range of policy options that were approved of during the early years of the Vietnam War (Verba et al., 1967). Majorities could be found for bombing North Vietnam (but not China) and for sending more U.S. troops, but also for negotiation and even for allowing Viet Cong participation in the South Vietnamese government. Americans may have been muddled or inconsistent in these judgments. Or they may have been expressing a desire to end the war, not necessarily by a clear-cut victory, and in effect giving the government a broad mandate to choose among various means to achieve that goal. Either tough or conciliatory actions, taken in moderation and appropriately timed by the government, would meet with approval by a majority. As it was, President Johnson chose to move primarily in the direction of military action but, if the survey data are to be believed, alternatively he could have built support for a negotiated settlement.

Much the same conclusions follow from the evidence for at least a short-term "rally 'round the flag" for almost anything that looks like decisive action in foreign affairs. Public opinion can endorse and legitimize a wide range of policies. During the Iran hostage crisis, a survey asked whether people would approve each of six hypothetical actions. One moderately conciliatory option (send the Shah elsewhere) was approved by 74 percent, and one—in context—moderately hawkish option (a naval blockade of Iran) approved by 62 percent. Moreover, people were asked, about all six actions, whether they would change their views "if President Carter considered this action necessary." On the average, about half of those initially opposed said they would change. Similar responses about yielding to presidential judgment appeared in a Utah survey among residents opposed to Reagan administration plans to base the MX missile there (Sigelman, 1980; Edwards, 1983). Not surprisingly, willingness to defer to presidential judgment is greater for those who already are partisans of the president (Mueller, 1973).

The possibilities of leadership even on such a hotly disputed issue as "peace for territory" in Israel are shown by a 1973 question that asked whether people would "support a peace agreement that involves giving up most of the territories." At first, 45 percent said yes. But when the proviso "if the government supports it" was added, those who would agree rose to 54 percent. Symmetrically, the phrase "if the government is against it" dropped support down to 36 percent.[2] In two surveys in early 1989, the percentage of the population willing to allow Palestinians to hold local elections jumped by 17 points after Prime Minister Yitzhak Shamir endorsed a similar plan. An extreme example of the rally effect appeared in answer to the question, "Do you believe it is essential, or not, to support a government during a security crisis, like war, even when one does not agree with what it is doing?" to which 88 percent said yes (Arian, 1977; *Foreign Opinion Note,* 1989; Arian et al., 1989).

Among Arab Palestinians in the occupied territories, "a binational state in the whole of Palestine" was acceptable to the largest proportion (64 percent), but also rated as acceptable to a majority were both the extreme "Palestinian state in the whole of Palestine with expulsion of the Jews" (53 percent) and the more moderate "Jordan-Palestinian state that lives in peace next to Israel within the 1967 borders" (54 percent). Nearly half (45 percent) even were willing to make "border modifications in accordance with Israel's security needs." This was before both the intifada and PLO chairman Yasser Arafat's endorsement of

2. A formula of giving up *some* territory for peace, but without specifying any kind of Palestinian state, came by 1988 and especially 1989 to be approved by a solid Israeli majority. See E. Katz, 1989; *Foreign Opinion Note,* 1989.

some kind of a two-state settlement (Inbar and Yuchtman-Yaar, 1989).

Toughness and negotiation are not mutually exclusive. One can "bargain from strength": be firm and unyielding right up to the last moment and then offer a major concession—a recognized negotiating strategy. Elements of both are in fact widely advocated by the same individuals. In a response to a survey question frequently asked by the Roper Organization, typically one-fourth of the population chose, "It's clear Russia can't be trusted and we will have to rely on increased military strength to counter them"; another one-fourth answered, "We should do nothing that is likely to provoke an American-Russian conflict but instead try to negotiate and reason out our differences"; and about half essentially combined the two: "We should take a strong position with the Russians now so they won't go any further but at the same time we should try to re-establish good relations with them" (Schneider, 1987, p. 49; Schneider, 1984; Free and Cantril, 1967; in Western Europe, Flynn and Rattinger, 1985; Eichenberg, 1989). When announcing the American attack on Viet Cong "sanctuaries" in Cambodia, President Nixon tried (unsuccessfully), with a carefully crafted speech, to present his action as centrist, neither an invasion of Cambodia nor a pullout.

Most foreign policy actions, even those toward the center, will offend those at one end or the other of the range of opinions. But the Iran-Contra affair had the unusual capability of offending the entire range. It had a disastrous effect on President Reagan's popularity (an immediate 20-point drop in his job performance index in the polls, with only a modest recovery thereafter) because it offended both ends of the hawk-dove spectrum. Two-thirds of the population, including but not limited to the dovish left, opposed giving military assistance to the Nicaraguan contras. But the secret dealings with Iran angered equal numbers, including many on the hawkish right. Iran's popularity rating among twenty-three countries was down at the bottom, well below even Syria and the Soviet Union (Schneider, 1987, pp. 56–57, 60). Elite criticism of either element was therefore safe. Also, the acts themselves were mixed. One was a conciliatory move toward a hated adversary (Iran); the other was a step up the escalation ladder of military force in Central America.

Finally, military action to repel an armed attack across international borders more effectively rallies support than does military intervention against domestic communists within a country. The 1983 action against Grenada was more widely accepted when presented as "mainly to protect the Americans living there" than when presented as to overthrow a Marxist government (Schneider, 1987, p. 59; earlier, Mueller, 1977). In 1986, the Nicaraguan government was posing no immediate threat to its neighbors or to the United States, so American popular sentiment to overthrow it was low.

Nuclear Weapons: Being Tough but Keeping the Risks Down

The preferred mix of toughness and conciliation varies for many reasons, but usually with some discernible consistency, internal logic, and relation to external events. It evolves as conditions in the world at large evolve. Over the history of the post–World War II era, support for the use of military force—including nuclear weapons—was strongest when the United States had the clearest advantage. Immediately after the war, about 80 percent of the population approved the use of nuclear weapons against Japan. (Indeed, a vengeful 23 percent said, "We should have quickly used many more of them before Japan had a chance to surrender.") Now, in retrospect, the approvers number between a little over half to two-thirds of the population (Graham, 1989b, pp. 43, 45, 83).

Loss of the nuclear monopoly in 1949 made little immediate difference, perhaps because the public generally understood that the Soviet Union did not yet have any means to deliver bombs against American targets. The questions that show the greatest readiness to use nuclear weapons first in a possible war are both distinct for their wording. In 1949 the populace rejected by almost three to one the proposition that "the United States should pledge that we will never use the atom bomb in warfare until some other nation has used it on us"—but the question implies a unilateral American pledge rather than a mutual one. Two years later, two-thirds of the population said that if the United States should get into an all-out war with Russia "we should use atomic bombs first" rather than "only if used on us" (19 percent)—but the phrase "all-out war" partially prejudges the case by suggesting an inevitability that the bombs will be used on us anyway (Erskine, 1963). Less tilted questions produced approval of first use of nuclear weapons nearer the 50 percent level.

The intensified cold war, and the Korean War, marked the greatest readiness to use nuclear weapons, but even then this readiness was hardly overwhelming. In 1950 about half the population expressed a willingness to use them in response to a Soviet attack on Western Europe; this dropped a little but still remained over 40 percent in 1956. Similar opinions applied in consideration of a communist attack in Asia. Variants of this question were asked often in the early and middle 1950s, and answers ranged from below 30 percent to above 60 percent depending on the wording. The average such response on a survey was around 45 percent; that is, about the same level as within Western Europe itself. A small majority also was prepared to use the bomb in Korea, against the Chinese (Graham, 1989b).

In the early 1950s it still was possible for many to believe that the United States was relatively immune to Soviet nuclear retaliation. Although, by 1950, 60 to 80 percent of the population thought that the atom bomb would be used against the United States if a war (or world war) should occur—a figure that has remained in that range ever since—in 1951, 42 percent thought they "would feel reasonably safe if an atomic war should come" (50 percent not safe). And although most people expected nuclear weapons to be used in any attack on the United States, in 1952 and 1954 three-fourths of those with an opinion thought that no more than a few enemy planes would get through, and only a third thought that their own community would be hit (Withey, 1954; Erskine, 1963). These perceptions were not far from those held by government leaders at the time (see, e.g., Betts, 1987).

Expectations of personal vulnerability rose as the Soviet Union acquired first a bomber force capable of hitting the United States on roundtrip missions, and then a force of intercontinental ballistic missiles. As early as 1956 a majority of Americans with opinions thought that the area where they lived would be wiped out, and that they and their families would not be likely to live through an atomic war. By 1963, the "don't knows" had shrunk from 32 percent to 8 percent, and a majority (52 percent) thought their chances of surviving would be poor (Erskine, 1963; Kramer et al., 1983; Graham, 1989b). That percentage has continued to rise somewhat, as Americans have absorbed a belief in MAD (mutual assured destruction) as a reality whatever the official policy characterizations. By 1987, 83 percent thought there could be no limited nuclear war; that a nuclear war would become all-out and all mankind would be destroyed (Yankelovich and Harman, 1988, pp. 49, 64; Smith, 1988).

At the same time, public enthusiasm for using nuclear weapons—never overwhelming—has dropped. Since the late 1950s readiness to use nuclear weapons to defend Europe or Asia has hovered generally in a range of from 15 to 40 percent depending on question wording, only rarely going outside that range. The average level is about 30 percent as a means of defending Europe, and 20 percent for Asia, consistent with experts' general assessment of the former's greater strategic importance. Save for a dip in the late 1960s and a short-term peak in the early 1980s, there are no significant shifts over time after 1956. This low percentage contrasts with a much higher commitment to the defense of allies in general. If nuclear weapons are not mentioned, but Americans are simply asked whether they are willing to defend allies with military force, the percentages in the affirmative are much higher (between 60 and 75 percent for defending Western Europe) and have risen in the last decade. The same support remains in place for maintaining American troops in Europe, at least as of 1982 (Russett and DeLuca, 1981; Flynn et al., 1985, pp. 72–78; Graham, 1989b, appendix 1).

As for whether use of the atomic bombs against Japan was, in retrospect, a good thing, the average response since 1950 has been between 60 and 70 percent affirmative, again with no clear trend once the immediate support level of 80 percent had dropped. Most Americans still believe the alternative was an invasion of the Japanese home islands with hundreds of thousands of American casualties—a belief many members of the foreign policy elite continue to hold, despite evidence that President Truman and his advisers had *much* lower contemporary estimates of the likely toll in American lives (Bernstein, 1987).

One trend, however, is quite clear. As Figure 3.1 shows, in the 1940s about 60 percent of Americans believed that development of the atomic bomb was overall "a good thing," and only a third held the contrary opinion. But by the 1970s the doubters out-

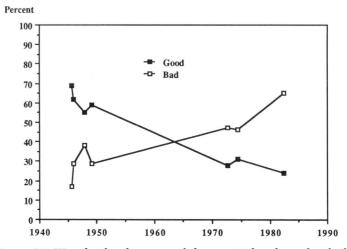

Figure 3.1. Was the development of the atomic bomb good or bad?
Source: Data from Small, 1989.

numbered the enthusiasts, and by 1982 two-thirds of the population said it had been bad, and only a quarter considered it good (Small, 1989). Attitudes toward nuclear weapons now share many characteristics of those toward nuclear power—not clear-cut opposition, but ambivalence; regarding them as part of a devil's bargain bringing irresistible benefits but also implying the risk of horrendous long-term costs (Gamson and Modigliani, 1989).

Another indication of changing popular perception of the bomb emerges in the diminished support for building additional nuclear weapons. It is hard to evaluate this over a decades-long period because the nature of the weapons systems changes, and many of the survey questions refer to particular weapons (neutron bomb, MX, B-1 bomber) about which some controversy raged. Nevertheless, general questions about the desirability of building more nuclear weapons are identifiable from the period 1946–1950, and after a gap again for the mid-1980s. As Figure 3.2 shows, whereas more nuclear weapons regularly commanded majority support in the early cold war years, by 1982 the conviction that the United States had enough was dominant. Save for a brief resurgence of interest in more weapons that coincided with the 1984 election, a solid majority of the population regu-

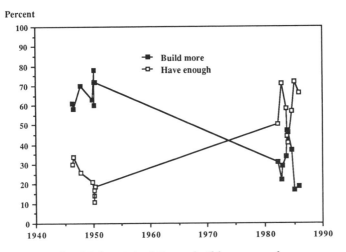

Figure 3.2. Should the United States build more nuclear weapons? Source: Data from Small, 1989.

Table 3.1. American attitudes toward nuclear disarmament.

Attitudes toward	Percentages		
	Favor	Oppose	No opinion
U.S.–USSR agreement to destroy all existing nuclear weapons	47	44	9
U.S.–USSR agreement to build no more nuclear weapons	72	20	8
Of the 60 percent of respondents who think the USSR "not at all likely" to abide by an agreement	65	28	7
If a UN-sponsored referendum, would vote for nuclear disarmament	59	29	12

Source: Data from *Gallup Report*, May 1981, pp. 3–9.

larly recorded themselves as satisfied with the existing level (Small, 1989).

As Table 3.1 shows, even many people who expected the Russians to cheat said they would favor an agreement to build no more. Pluralities or majorities disapproved of the Reagan administration's decision to abandon the SALT II treaty, thought the decision would increase the chances of war and decrease the chances to reach future arms agreements, and thought it would increase the arms race (*Gallup Report,* June 1986).

Most Americans remain committed to nuclear deterrence, if with many reservations. In a 1984 Public Agenda survey 62 percent rejected the idea that "by the 1990s it should be American policy never to use nuclear weapons under any conditions." They think that nuclear weapons have helped to keep the peace, and according to a 1982 survey were willing, by a two-to-one margin, to *risk* destruction of the United States rather than be dominated by the Soviet Union (Kohut, 1988; my emphasis). They have some qualms about this. For instance, in 1977 a Harris Poll found 52 percent believing it was morally wrong for a country to use nuclear weapons "even if it has to," and the Public Agenda found 79 percent agreeing that "there is nothing on earth that could ever justify the all-out use of nuclear weapons." But "an eye for an eye"; that is, nuclear retaliation for a nuclear attack against us, retains the support of from 65 to 90 percent of the population, depending on just how the question is asked.[3]

Nuclear weapons do give rise to moral ambiguity, and overall they probably are not considered to be a "good thing."[4] In the first decades of the cold war Americans believed—by a three-to-one margin, greater than in other industrialized democracies— that nuclear weapons decreased the chance of war. Now people are no longer so sure, with those who think the weapons decrease the chance of war only narrowly outnumbering those who think they increase it. Moreover, the social base of support has changed. In the early years the more highly educated elements of the population favored the weapons disproportionately; in the more recent period educational levels have rarely made much difference.

3. Here and elsewhere, if there is no specific citation to survey materials the data can be found in materials of the public opinion and arms control project at Yale University, directed by Thomas W. Graham and Bruce Russett, and usually in the Roper Center archives at Yale.

4. A 1985 survey about SDI is instructive. It contrasted a hypothetical system with "nuclear weapons in orbit, ready to be triggered from the ground . . ." against one "that would not involve nuclear devices but would consist of electromagnetic launchers, or 'rail guns,' on the ground," and asked respondents whether they would prefer the system with "the nuclear weapon or the non-nuclear weapon." The nonnuclear one won by more than six to one. Americans Talk Security, 1987, p. 268.

Yet the weapons exist, and at least so long as the Russians also have them they are seen as filling a deterrent function that most Americans are unwilling to forgo. Certainly they are unwilling to forgo the use of nuclear weapons in response to a (really pretty implausible) Soviet conventional attack on the United States; their attitude toward the situation of a Soviet conventional attack on one of America's principal allies is more equivocal (Small, 1989; Graham, 1989b).

Limited use of nuclear weapons in response to a Soviet conventional attack on NATO allies in Europe is the kind of "first use" that most Americans would be reluctant to forswear unilaterally. Nevertheless, the lack of enthusiasm shows, as most Americans regularly favor a no-first-use *agreement* with the Soviet Union. (A no-first-use agreement, if both sides thought it might be kept, of course would diminish the value of American nuclear weapons for deterring a conventional attack in Europe. Most Americans may think that is an acceptable price.) From 1950 to 1960 roughly 60 percent of the population favored such an agreement, and that number rose to about 70 percent by the 1980s. Indeed, a survey at that time found 81 percent believing—erroneously—that it was official American policy not to use nuclear weapons first (Kramer et al., 1983; Yankelovich and Doble, 1984, p. 45).[5] The precise distribution of responses varies over time, and with the wording of the question, but so long as the principle of a bilateral agreement is at issue, and not a unilateral renunciation, public endorsement is clear.

The reality of mutual nuclear deterrence, plus perhaps the articulation of deterrence theory, has been understood by the public; high-income and high-education groups do not differ notably from the public in general. This means that Soviet nuclear weapons themselves are not necessarily considered to be so bad. In 1950, two surveys asked whether, now that the Soviet Union had the bomb, the chances of war would increase or decrease. Many people did not think the Soviet bomb made a difference; of those who did, by about three to two they saw the chances of war rising. But as Figure 3.3 shows, by the middle 1950s and

5. This is sensitive to question wording, however; with some formulations the percentage erroneously believing no-first-use is official policy drops to 47. Americans Talk Security, January 1989, p. 75.

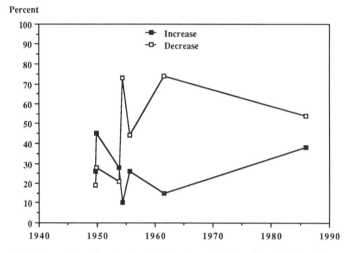

Figure 3.3. Now that the Soviet Union has the bomb, will the chances of war decrease, increase, or stay the same? Source: Data from Small, 1989.

early 1960s perceptions had changed dramatically—to the point where by about a three-to-one margin they saw the changes of war as *decreasing* with the Soviet bomb. This continued to be the majority opinion in the 1980s, though by a narrower margin than earlier. By about a four-to-one margin Americans have for many years consistently believed that the United States possesses a "second strike" capability to retaliate for any nuclear attack; when asked in the 1980s whether the Soviet Union also had such a capability, a strong majority said that they did (Small, 1989).

Americans' acceptance of the fact and theory of mutual deterrence shows in response to repeated questions about whether they prefer the United States to be stronger, weaker, or equal to the Soviet Union in nuclear weapons. Until the early 1980s Americans regularly expressed a preference for American nuclear strength to exceed that of the Soviet Union. But beginning in 1983 most surveys have found a substantial majority saying only that they wished the United States to be equal, and in doing so they joined a long-held position of most West Europeans (Russett and DeLuca, 1983; Small, 1989). They seek a balance of power, not advantage or dominance. Of course few (only about 10 percent) wanted the United States to be weaker. But consistently fewer than 25 percent wanted the United States to be superior, and about 60 percent said that of the three options they preferred the United States and the Soviet Union to have equal power.

Also, equal power is all they saw as feasible. When a Gallup survey of March 1987 asked whether further increases in nuclear weapons could give the United States or the Soviet Union a real advantage over the other, 69 percent said they could not and only 21 percent thought they could. (Americans Talk Security, 1987, p. 239). The Public Agenda project (1988) reported that, by March 1988, 83 percent said "If we had a bigger nuclear arsenal than the Soviets, they would keep building until they caught up."

Overall, we see in these survey responses a rather sophisticated and coherent understanding of the basic principles which many mainstream nuclear strategists have been trying to convey. Americans are not eager either to surrender vital global positions or to "nuke" their major adversaries.

The Balance of Attitudes in Western Europe

Western Europeans have long accepted the principles of mutual deterrence. Since the middle of the 1960s, repeated samplings in the larger European countries (Britain, France, Germany, Italy) have almost always shown about a two-to-one preference for Soviet-American parity rather than for American superiority. This has been true for the mass public as well as for the elites, and the reason is simple: parity implies mutual deterrence and caution; superiority implies the possibility of recklessness and adventurism. Europeans prefer that neither side have confidence it can "win" a world war or a European war (Russett and DeLuca, 1983, p. 191).

European attitudes toward American nuclear weapons in Europe have been ambivalent. At the height of the controversy over the intended deployment of American Pershing II and cruise missiles in Western Europe, Europeans were divided in their beliefs about the effect of the missiles. A plurality in Britain (farthest from the front lines) thought the weapons "increased the chances of attack" rather than "provided greater protection."

In France and West Germany, however, a plurality favored "greater protection," and in Belgium those two camps were about evenly split while half the population had no opinion or thought the missiles had no effect. American *troops* stationed in Western Europe were far more welcome than nuclear weapons. As the perceived threat of deliberate Soviet attack recedes toward the vanishing point, nuclear weapons themselves are seen as the overriding cause of war. Nuclear weapons are tolerated for deterrence so long as their possessors are seen as responsible; loose talk about "limited" nuclear war frightens Europeans badly (Russett and DeLuca, 1983; for Japan see Bobrow, 1989).

Even 60 percent of the Dutch believed, in 1982, that nuclear weapons had helped to preserve the peace in Europe, and 43 percent said that NATO would have to continue to depend on them for deterrence. Europeans are not pacifists. If asked whether "war is so horrible" it would be "better to accept Russian domination rather than to risk war," or whether "it would be better to fight in defense of your country than to accept Russian domination," majorities ranging from six to one (Britain) to three to one (Italy) chose "fight" (Flynn et al., 1985, p. 31; Domke et al., 1987, p. 395; Rattinger, 1987).

But opposition to the actual use of nuclear weapons is even stronger and more apparent in Western Europe than in the United States—not surprisingly, because Europe's density of population and its position on the front lines of East-West rivalry ensure that any actual use of nuclear weapons there would have immeasurable destructive effects. That opposition has increased recently, but it has long been present. For more than three decades surveys have consistently reported extreme skepticism about fighting a "limited" nuclear war in Europe. Save for a couple of surveys in Britain at the very beginning of that time, in the ten countries surveyed there has almost never been net approval (percentage approving minus percentage disapproving) of a first use of nuclear weapons *"even if a Soviet attack by conventional forces threatened to overwhelm NATO forces."* The longer NATO has relied on a threat of first use—and the less credible that threat has become with the loss of Western strategic nuclear superiority—the more negative European attitudes have become. The use of nuclear weapons is approved by a majority only if the Soviets use them first (Capitanchik and Eichenberg,

1983; Kramer et al., 1983; Russett and DeLuca, 1983; de Boer, 1984; Flynn et al., 1985, ch. 4; den Oudsten, 1988).[6]

About 40 percent of Europeans could accurately be called "nuclear pacifists," that is, opposed to using nuclear weapons under any circumstances. This is higher than in the United States (but lower than in Japan, which has about 60 percent) because so few Europeans (fewer than one in ten) believe that they personally would survive a nuclear war (Adler, 1986).

European governments nevertheless remain committed to nuclear deterrence; indeed, more committed to nuclear deterrence of war in Europe than are American elites. The no-first-use heresy expressed by Americans McGeorge Bundy, George Kennan, Robert McNamara, and Gerard Smith (1982)[7] has been almost uniformly rejected by the European national security establishment. Why?

First, many Europeans do in some sense accept the principles of "existential deterrence." They would not want to have nuclear weapons used, in any way whatever, in a war—but they think the mere existence and deployment of nuclear weapons makes war very unlikely. In some sense this may seem like a "bluff" deterrent, one that an adversary could readily see through. (After all, if the Europeans wouldn't actually use the weapons, why should the Soviets be deterred by the mere existence of them?) But this is not silly. There is always some nontrivial chance that the weapons will be used whether or not the Europeans want

6. Israel represents a limiting case, the state hardest pressed economically by defense burdens and most exposed if attacked by a determined and capable enemy. Yet even there, popular sentiment for using nuclear weapons is hardly enthusiastic. In answer to "Are there circumstances in which it would be justified for Israel to use nuclear weapons (if it has or will have these weapons), or do you believe that under no circumstances should nuclear weapons be used?" the ayes had it by only 53 percent to 47 percent. When probed, popular willingness is limited to major provocations: "in response to a nuclear attack" (96 percent of those willing to use nuclear weapons at all), "in a state of absolute helplessness" (53 percent), or "to save many lives" (52), but not "to save a small number of lives" (21), or "as a warfare tactic, instead of mobilizing the regular army" (13). See Arian et al., 1989.

7. By the 1980s large portions of the U.S. national security elite, including admirals and generals, had reached a similar conclusion. Kohut and Horrock, 1984, report that a survey of such flag officers found 61 percent saying they could not justify a nuclear first strike against the Soviet Union. To be sure, despite ambiguities, in strategic parlance "no first strike," which might permit small-scale demonstrative uses not constituting an "attack," implies a less restrictive policy than does "no first use."

them to be. The American government may give the order, or some lower-level commander, in the heat of battle and fog of war, may be able to use them. Presumably the Soviet leaders know this, and can be deterred by it. If Soviet leaders think that the probability of "inadvertent" use of nuclear weapons after a conventional attack is high, and if they have little incentive to attack anyway, that may be all that matters.[8] And Europeans do have generally lower perceptions than Americans that war is likely (see below), and a somewhat less alarmist view of Soviet intentions providing that Western countries pursue nonprovocative policies.

Second, the cost-benefit ratio is different for Europeans than for Americans. For them, conventional (nonnuclear) war is little more attractive than nuclear war. Many Europeans remember the last conventional war on the continent and have no desire to repeat the experience. Abandoning the nuclear deterrent might very well raise the attractions of conventional war to an aggressor. If the odds of war go up a lot, and the degree of "damage limitation" improves only moderately, the switch is a bad bargain.

Furthermore, nuclear weapons are relatively cheap, and whether people actually would be prepared to spend more to strengthen conventional (nonnuclear) defenses is at best open to question. Inquiries in Britain produced about an even split between those who say they would be willing to spend more for conventional weapons in order to rely less on nuclear ones and those who say they would not—a split not terribly sensitive to question wording (Russett and DeLuca, 1983). Especially given the commitment of European voters to expensive elements of the welfare state, few European leaders have been willing to try seriously to make the trade. European governments seem to be willing to improve conventional defense just barely to whatever level is required to maintain the presence of American forces on the continent, and no further.

Americans do not face the clear nonnuclear threat to themselves that confronts Europeans, and hence are more willing to

---

8. Many American military experts see this situation as desirable; e.g. Bracken, 1988. Others, including myself, would prefer to see command and control over nuclear weapons in Europe kept very tight.

consider conventional defense. In the United States, two-thirds have said they would be willing to pay higher taxes if both America and Russia would reduce nuclear weapons and replace them with nonnuclear forces (Yankelovich and Doble, 1984, p. 45). The strength of such sentiments is in doubt, however, because people are much more willing to say that they will spend more for something in the abstract than if they are faced with an explicit list of tradeoffs (Mueller, 1977, pp. 324–325). Their true willingness is hard to measure with survey instruments. Political leaders basically have assumed that this particular tradeoff would be unacceptable. But because so few leaders have tried to persuade Western citizens to pay more to reduce reliance on nuclear weapons, the real degree of popular willingness remains unknown. With the recent easing of East-West tensions the prospect exists for reduction of both kinds of military spending.

Finally, European and American political systems are different in a major respect. Western European governments, accustomed to life in the vortex of power politics, have tried to keep their foreign and security policies well insulated from popular passions. Since the end of World War II they have maintained a remarkably stable policy of adherence to the Atlantic alliance while steadily seeking to move toward more normal relations with their communist neighbors. They know they have much to lose from a misstep, and, despite sporadic flourishes of rhetoric from the left, on the whole their populaces are willing to accept this degree of insulation. By contrast, European leaders see American security policy as more subject to changes in popular modes and therefore as more unstable. They recoiled from the saber-rattling rhetoric of the early Reagan years less because they really saw the American government as more dangerous than because they feared it might upset their own people. Also— especially in West Germany—they saw that rhetoric and possible Soviet reaction as a threat to their own policy of Ostpolitik. For West Germans it was particularly important to open trading opportunities in Eastern Europe and personal contacts with other Germans in the Democratic Republic. Residual fears from this period, plus the Gorbachev-led subsequent warming of East-West relations, produced serious resistance, even in the conservative Christian Democratic government, to modernization of short-range NATO nuclear forces in Germany (Domke et al., 1987; Mueller and Risse-Kappen, 1987).

Mutual Agreement, Not Unilateral Concessions

The delicate American support for no-first-use of nuclear weapons—in favor of a mutual agreement on it with the Soviets, ambivalent about actual first use in war, but against a unilateral renunciation of first use—illustrates the fundamental "centrism" of most American opinion on security issues. Yet another illustration is from the politics of the nuclear test ban in the 1950s and 1960s. In the 1956 presidential election, Adlai Stevenson campaigned for an end to American nuclear testing—sometimes with an explicit call for a unilateral cessation by the United States, and sometimes simply without explicitly asking for a joint U.S.–Soviet agreement. His urgings fell flat. It was partly that the public had not yet come to perceive nuclear fallout as a very serious problem, but Stevenson's unilateralist approach would have condemned him anyway. The public later became more concerned, and President Eisenhower initiated a unilateral cessation of American testing. This action still was not approved by a majority, but it was accepted because of Eisenhower's perceived military expertise, and because he was seen as more realistic on security matters than Stevenson (Graham, 1989a, ch. 5).

Here, as we shall see repeatedly, a leader perceived as "hawkish" can successfully take "dovish" initiatives that the public would reject from a "dovish" leader. If he is far ahead of the public, however, bureaucratic and domestic political pressures will build against him. John Kennedy—despite the cover given him by the largely hawkish position he had staked out in decrying the "missile gap" and by talking tougher about Cuba than Richard Nixon did—could not contain the pressures to resume U.S. nuclear testing. But when he finally concluded a *bilateral agreement* with Nikita Khrushchev to cease atmospheric testing, public endorsement was ready, as it had been for several years.

The phrase "unilateral disarmament" contains one dubious word and one clearly bad one. "Disarmament" is already suspect, because of the general existential acceptance of deterrence in a realist's world of competing states. On the one hand, given the widespread ambivalence about nuclear weapons, "nuclear disarmament" may seem desirable. The nuclear freeze movement was supported across a wide variety of groups with divergent attitudes on other issues; as long as the question was asked (through 1984) a mutual and verifiable freeze commanded 75 to 80 percent approval (Milburn et al., 1986). It was partly to counter the freeze that President Reagan presented SDI as a way to make nuclear deterrence obsolete, and both he and Gorbachev have struck resonant chords with their calls to abolish all nuclear weapons.

But whereas in the abstract many forms of disarmament may seem desirable, in practice people take the term as connoting unilateral action. And unilateral is the really bad word. "Reduction" (especially of nuclear weapons) is much more attractive by lacking this connotation associated with disarmament. "Agreement," "negotiation," "inspection," and "verification" connote important contrasts to unilateralism.

As Table 3.1 showed, there is some readiness to take chances that the Soviets will cheat, and this readiness has risen. A decade or so ago 74 percent of Americans said that "unless the Soviets agree to on-site inspection, we should refuse to sign any arms control agreements with them" (Adler, 1986). As late as 1986 and 1987, two-thirds said the Soviets "lie, cheat, and steal," and 50 percent asserted "the U.S. shouldn't sign any agreements for arms control" because "the Soviets will not keep their end of the bargain" (Hinckley, 1989). Yet in January 1985 a 76 percent majority agreed that "the United States should negotiate a nuclear arms limitation agreement even if there is risk that the Soviets would cheat." Whereas 81 percent of those familiar with the SALT II treaty believed the Soviet Union had not lived up to its terms, 53 percent believed the United States had not done so either. Instead of putting the blame for cheating entirely on the Soviet Union, 73 percent of Americans agreed that "both the U.S. and the Soviets cheat on treaties to some extent; it's just part of the game" (Schneider, 1987; *Gallup Report,* June 1986; Americans Talk Security, 1987, p. 215).[9]

9. In Britain at about this time the pox-on-both-houses view was even stronger. Asked whether the Soviets "can be trusted to keep to their agreements on nuclear

By 1987 the balance between believing that the greater risk in an arms control agreement was in trusting the Soviets too much (43 percent) and believing that the greater risk lay in being too suspicious to enter into an agreement at all (41 percent) was about even. And by January 1988 the level of trust had risen and become nonpartisan. Of Republicans and Democrats respectively, 43 and 44 percent said the Soviet Union "can be trusted" to keep its part of the new INF treaty, over 60 percent of both said the United States can trust the Soviet Union at least somewhat, and more than 70 percent of both expressed a willingness to trust Gorbachev in particular. President Reagan's own apparent shift in attitude brought many Republicans along after him (Morin, 1988).

The American public still, however, treats unilateral disarmament moves on the part of the Soviet Union with some skepticism, not surprisingly given its long-held suspicion of Soviet intentions and its conviction about the need for verification of arms control steps. Unilateral action may become more acceptable in light of several Gorbachev initiatives in recent years, including his long unilateral suspension of all Soviet nuclear testing and his subsequent troop reductions in Europe and actions to dispose of chemical weapons stocks.

Many advocates of arms control welcome the Soviet actions and would like to see a reciprocal policy by the United States. They envisage a kind of tit-for-tat exchange of actions without prior negotiation: I make a unilateral concession, and then I look to see if you do something more or less equivalent. If so, then I move with another concession. This process, known sometimes as GRIT (gradual reduction of international tensions) is attractive because it bypasses the tedious and tangled process of negotiating equivalent concessions between the two superpowers. It was practiced successfully by Kennedy and Khrushchev in 1963, before Kennedy's assassination (Osgood, 1962; Etzioni, 1967; Russett, 1983b, ch. 7). But the prompt, verifiable reciprocation of all concessions and agreements is important, perhaps more important to the broad political acceptability of arms control and disarmament than to the actual military importance of ver-

---

arms," Britons split 64 percent no to 22 percent yes, and trust of the United States little better, 56 percent no and 30 percent yes. See Sabin, 1986/87.

ification and inspection in the eyes of many experts.[10] So too is the verbal packaging: "independent initiatives" sounds much better than unilateral disarmament.

Bargaining from Equality: Confidence and Fear

Trust alone remains far too insubstantial a basis for renewed Soviet-American détente. If most Americans do not seek superiority in nuclear arms, neither are they ready to accept the implications of inferiority. In 1987 they were split evenly on whether "the continued arms race" or "falling behind the Soviets" was the greater threat to peace. If the arms race is a danger and not something America can hope to win, neither is it something the United States can afford to lose (Kohut, 1988; Yankelovich and Harman, 1988). Moreover, Americans are readier to embrace arms control and disarmament at times when they feel the United States is not inferior. The Reagan years illustrate this well, and the attitude is likely to be reinforced by Reagan's rhetoric about achieving the INF cuts only because the United States bargained from a position of strength. At a time (1987 and 1988) when most Americans opposed further increases in military spending, 58 percent or more nevertheless felt that the Reagan buildup had been necessary. Reagan's leadership ratings were higher for his handling of defense and Soviet-American relations than were his general ratings (Martilla, 1989, pp. 280, 313).

In 1980 Americans were asked whether they preferred a policy emphasizing arms strength, or one of a mixture of strength and negotiation. The policy of strength was preferred two to one. In the first two years of the Reagan administration the polls found strong endorsement of a "get tough" policy; fewer than one American in five wanted a "conciliatory" negotiating approach. But by 1988, with the same questions, only one in five advocated getting tough and two-thirds supported a reduction of tensions. And by 1987 the choice on strength or a mixture of negotiation and strength had shifted to 56 percent in favor of the latter. The

10. On the INF agreement, for example, ACDA specialists regard normal means of U.S. intelligence gathering as much more important for verification than on-site inspection.

domestic and international political environments had changed in important ways. But perhaps the greatest difference stemmed from the military buildup during the interim. Two-thirds said that the buildup had been necessary—and 84 percent saw no need for any further buildup (Yankelovich and Smoke, 1988; Mandel, 1989).

In recent years most Americans have rarely perceived the United States as on balance ahead of the Soviet Union in nuclear strength, but neither have they often thought the United States was behind. As Figure 3.4 shows, most of the time 40 to 50 percent answered that the two countries were about even, and 30 percent or fewer saw the Soviet Union as ahead.[11] This was true even in the late 1970s during the deterioration of détente and the public relations effort by the Committee on the Present Danger to persuade the public that the United States had fallen behind. The public accepted the characterization of American inferiority only in the brief period between 1980 and 1983 fol-

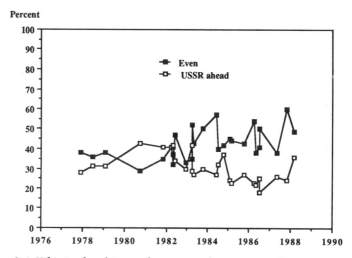

Figure 3.4. Who is ahead in nuclear strength: Russia or the United States, or are they about even? Source: Data from Small, 1989.

11. They have been somewhat more likely to see the Soviets as ahead in conventional weaponry—in agreement with the opinion of experts that the Soviet military advantage is greater in nonnuclear forces than nuclear ones. The British and French publics (and to a lesser degree the West German and Italian) have long had stronger perceptions than Americans that the Soviet Union was ahead militarily. See Russett and DeLuca, 1983, p. 190.

lowing the events in Iran and Afghanistan. During those years the percentage seeing the two rivals as even often dropped into the thirties, and 40 percent or more believed the Soviets to be ahead (Small, 1989). Whether or not that was an accurate representation of the nuclear balance at the time, it faithfully reflected the rhetoric of the first Reagan presidential campaign and of the new administration's call for a buildup of American arms. Many people accepted the administration's assessment, and while they did so they were less receptive to calls for arms control negotiations.

Subsequently the proportion of the population seeing the nuclear balance as even rose to about half, and those seeing the Russians as ahead dropped usually to under 30 percent. From that perspective negotiated arms limitation or reduction looked better. Cynicism and mistrust are associated with fear, greater trust with greater self-confidence. Public willingness to negotiate arms control agreements does not seem to require a sense of military superiority—fortunately, since that would likely provoke resistance from the Soviet side because of *their* perceptions of inferiority.

Many in the peace activist movement have simply not understood that fear is an unpredictable and often perverse motivator of action. They have often assumed that if people could be sufficiently alarmed about the likelihood and consequences of nuclear war, they would demand disarmament and arms control. But it has not worked that way. Fear of world war peaked in the United States during the Korean War period—hardly a dovish era, and one when support for military spending was also high. It then declined—a decline enhanced by the "lesson" of the Cuban missile crisis that we won because we were strong—and stayed relatively low until the early 1980s when, in common with opinion in virtually all countries, it peaked again. According to a Gallup (AIPO) survey in June 1981, 47 percent of the American populace thought that a nuclear war was likely in the subsequent ten years, and 60 percent said that they did not expect they personally would survive such a war.

Although those thinking a nuclear war to be probable were somewhat in the minority, they nevertheless at all times constituted a larger proportion of the population than in almost any other country for which we have public opinion data. The pop-

ulace of the United States consistently ranked among the top
two or three out of about thirty countries surveyed, sometimes
matched by white South Africans. (European countries typically
showed only 20 percent thinking war likely, despite being much
closer to Soviet military might. This probably says something
about the psychic costs of the cold war to its principal Western
protagonist.) Fears remained high in the United States as late as
March 1988, dropping sharply only in a May 1989 survey. They
were much higher in the mass public than among elites, nega-
tively correlated with education and socioeconomic status
(Mueller, 1979; de Boer, 1981, p. 131; *Gallup Report,* December
1986, p. 6; Russett and Lackey, 1987; Americans Talk Security
surveys, 1987–1989).[12]

During the early 1980s many people did support the idea of a
freeze—mutual and verifiable—on nuclear weapons. But they
also strongly supported an arms buildup, their fear rooted in a
sense of military inferiority. Support for greater military spending was at a twenty-five-year high from 1979 to 1982; the majority of Americans saw it as a means of deterring war rather than
as a provocation. Support for higher military spending, as well
as fear of war, was also higher among Americans than anywhere
else. (Russett and Starr, 1989, ch. 9) The widely viewed and
frightening film *The Day After* had little effect in changing
people's views on what to do about the threat of nuclear war;
after seeing it they split between arms control/disarmament and
"peace through strength" largely according to their earlier predispositions.

The uncertainties of fear-inducing communications have long
been recognized among psychologists, beginning with some
experimental work on how best to motivate people to brush
their teeth. Psychological mechanisms for dealing with fears
include not only vigilance and adaptive coping, but hypervigil-
ance, evasion, buck-passing, and "bolstering" (a form of "looking
on the bright side"; Janis and Mann, 1977). The trick is to produce a moderate amount of concern (or fear), but not so much
as to induce people simply to avoid thinking or acting about the

12. Whatever the overt wording of the question, it may well be that elites answer
in terms of a shorter time horizon (their own tenure in power, or their own lifetimes),
whereas members of the public implicitly consider their full lifetimes and those of
their children.

problem. Furthermore, people must be able clearly to envisage some effective action they can take; political activism on behalf of disarmament does not necessarily have this quality, especially at a time when the government in power exhibits every intention to resist the activists' pressure (Tyler and McGraw, 1983; Feshback and White, 1986).[13] Historians of postwar American culture agree that efforts to promote disarmament by frightening the population failed, and even backfired (Boyer, 1985; Weart, 1988).

Attitudes toward SDI (Strategic Defense Initiative, or "Star Wars") illustrate the effect of nuclear fears as well as popular ambivalence about nuclear weaponry. The principle of strategic defense has long been highly popular among Americans, and its approval is not much related to ideological position on other issues, or to perceptions of its cost or likely performance. In the terminology of the previous chapter, it is an issue of symbolic politics (Bobrow, 1969). Majorities or pluralities favored antiballistic missile (ABM) systems throughout the controversy during the Johnson and Nixon administrations; significantly, support was weakest near the end of the debate (1969) when the ability of ABM to protect cities became most questionable.

Many questions about SDI were asked from 1983 to 1988, and the results depend heavily on how the questions were phrased. Nevertheless, at least 50 percent of the population consistently favored it (even in the context of a nuclear freeze), with about 40 percent opposed and the rest undecided. People said they thought the United States should be doing more to protect people from nuclear attack. Popular support for SDI stemmed from real fears about the risks of nuclear war and the low probability of surviving it. Support was enhanced when SDI was referred to as Ronald Reagan's proposal, and varied directly with the degree to which SDI was seen as improving the prospects of survival, with 86 percent supporting "a system that was perfect and could successfully defend against all incoming nuclear weapons." (Between 50 and 75 percent thought—very contrary to fact—that the United States already had an effective defense.) Support for

13. Schuman et al., 1987, show that, save for the period 1983–86, Americans have not tended to cite the threat of nuclear war as one of the country's "most important problems," and that this is not sensitive to question wording. As they note, this can neither confirm nor refute the proposition that, by protective psychic denial, fears of war are kept largely below the surface of everyday consciousness.

a system preferred by many military experts—one "designed only to protect U.S. missiles, key military bases, and Washington, D.C., but not other areas"—dropped off to only 21 percent. Approval was reduced when questions referred to high costs or possible Soviet countermeasures (Graham and Kramer, 1986, p. 132–33; den Oudsten, 1986).

When continuing with SDI is offered as an obstacle to concluding other kinds of agreements with the Soviet Union the populace may split either way depending on how the question is worded and the strength of the arguments put forward (Public Agenda, 1988, p. 9). Approval of SDI went *up* in response to dovish arguments that it wouldn't work, or that the Soviet Union was hostile to it. Americans have faith in their technology, and retain a belief that if the Soviets don't like a thing it can't be all bad. Overall, attitudes on SDI are not rock-solid, and may change under different world conditions. SDI's proponents nevertheless tapped a deep vein of popular sentiment.

Fear of war may have corrosive effects on a broad range of attitudes and expectations. Psychiatrists have written about "psychic numbing" in the face of the nuclear danger (Lifton, ch. 8 in Lifton and Falk, 1982) and have concentrated especially on the effects of fears of nuclear war on American and Soviet children and adolescents. One author has declared, "It seems that these young people are growing up without . . . the sense of continuity upon which the development of stable personality structure and the formation of serviceable ideals depend. We may find we are raising generations of young people without a basis for making long-term commitments" (Mack, 1981, p. 20; Mack and Snow, 1986). Fears of war may even diminish people's willingness to save for the future. According to rational expectations theories of saving, people save largely in anticipation of their retirement, or to leave bequests. Beliefs (not necessarily conscious ones) that because of nuclear war they are unlikely to live to retirement or to have surviving progeny could be expected to diminish readiness to save. Some cross-national and cross-temporal analyses of national savings rates suggest this, as do some analyses of the attitudes and behavior of particular individuals. The evidence so far is inconclusive but intriguing (Slemrod, 1986; Hendershott and Peek, 1987; Russett and Lackey, 1987).

To the degree that people's fears of war are deep and pervasive, they become subject to manipulation by cynical or politically utopian promises, whether those promises be to abolish nuclear weapons from the earth or to create a leakproof "peace shield" (SDI). (According to Hertsgaard, 1988, Reagan aide Michael Deaver said he didn't know or care whether Star Wars would work, but supported it because it was "a great concept.") But the basic yearning for protection could also be mobilized to support serious arms reduction and arms control agreements. Nuclear weapons invoke vivid images for a form of symbolic politics, perhaps equivalent in foreign policy considerations to the Korean and Vietnam wars during their durations, and similar (though not necessarily as severe) to unemployment among domestic policy issues.

A Range of Choice for Soviet-American Relations

"While all Presidents are required both to stop the Soviets and to maintain peace, the imperatives are given different weights for Presidents of different parties" (Destler, et al., 1984, p. 49). Dwight Eisenhower could conclude a compromise peace to end the Korean war because he was widely respected as a general and a war hero. Richard Nixon, with his record of anticommunism, could renew relations with "Red China" and reach agreements for détente with the Soviet Union. Ronald Reagan, the most conservative president of the century, could get rapid ratification for his INF treaty after Jimmy Carter failed with SALT II. Elsewhere around the world one thinks readily of Charles de Gaulle, another general and war hero, ending the long French agony of the Algerian war, and of hard-liner Menachem Begin returning the Sinai peninsula to Egypt as part of a peace treaty. Of course one can readily produce counterexamples of perceived doves who nevertheless succeeded in dovish initiatives, and of hawks who never tried anything of the sort. Nevertheless, examples like the ones listed above are numerous enough, and important enough, to suggest a general pattern that cannot be ignored.

It is not just a matter of these dramatic events, however, or simply of a "hawkish" leader being able to get away with dovish acts politically. Harry Truman's 1948 campaigns for his party's nomination and then for the presidency combined a nice rhetorical balance of toughness and peace, bolstered by the "rally" effect in the Czechoslovakian and Berlin crises and protected from charges of being "soft on communism" by the left-wing candidacy of Henry Wallace (Divine, 1974). More generally, it is a matter of general expectations and the kind of freedom of action accorded to different kinds of leaders.

Whether accurately or as a reflection of his past rhetoric, almost any candidate for national leadership will be seen as in some degree toward the conservative or liberal end, the hawkish or dovish end, of political discourse. Leaders are elected by a majority vote; in political systems dominated by two major parties or two competing coalitions, the winner of any election will usually in some way represent *either* the right or the left. Yet in political systems where most voters are to be found somewhere within a broad center, candidates for national office will feel powerful pressures to draw their rhetoric and political appeal toward the center. (Some will of course do this more than others, but typically one sees at least a symbolic move to the center after the presidential nomination has been secured.) Because most voters are somewhere near the middle, they will be reassured when a president acts contrary to the ideological position they perceive him as holding. When he does so, he assures them that he is not far out of the central mainstream.

Miroslav Nincic (1988a) speaks of "the politics of opposites" in American foreign policy, well illustrated by the Carter and Reagan years. Jimmy Carter was widely perceived as a dove; when he talked or acted tough (as in the abortive attempt to rescue the hostages in Iran, or the post-Afghanistan sanctions against the Soviet Union) his approval rating rose. Ronald Reagan, by contrast, was seen as a hawk. His confrontational rhetoric was not so popular, and though the public approved his military action in Grenada they also approved his withdrawal of troops from Lebanon and negotiation of arms control with the Soviet Union. Carter's ratings systematically rose with tough actions; Reagan's with pacific ones. While few other presidents have had such clear "dovish" or "hawkish" public images as those two, the results suggest something important.

They suggest why President Reagan's political advisers, to the consternation of some senior military officers like General Bernard Rogers, counseled him to conclude a European nuclear arms control agreement (the INF treaty) at a time in 1987 when his popularity was badly faded. Not only is the public more willing to accept negotiated arms control at times when it feels more secure about its own country's military strength (as noted above), "the American public will be receptive to . . . arms control proposals of a president who it feels takes a harder line than it does" (Kohut, 1988, p. 65). As the next presidential election neared, a weakened Republican president could boost support for his party through an arms control agreement, a strategy much less effective for a Democratic president like Carter.

Does this mean that only hawkish presidents can act like doves and survive politically? That would be too strong an inference from recent experience. The Carter presidency, especially in the last two years, coincided with the decline of détente and, among the public, a growing concern that was a reaction to international events as well as to Carter's policies. His difficulty in continuing dovish policies was thus not surprising. And during the later years of the Reagan administration, the warming international climate, as well as Reagan's hawkish reputation, made his more moderate policies acceptable. Part of the difference between Carter's and Reagan's success with dovish policies was due to the skill of the latter's advisers in measuring the public pulse and tailoring the president's message to an acceptable mixture of toughness and conciliation.

Reagan's political advisers had already learned early in his presidency how to balance their packaging of a president who initially seemed too hawkish. When they warned him that, given rising public and congressional opposition, the Marines should be out of Lebanon well before the 1984 election campaign, he first said that House Speaker Tip O'Neill "may be ready to surrender, but I'm not." Yet the next day he "redeployed" the troops out to sea—while ordering a massive bombardment (Destler et al., 1984, p. 271; Powlick, 1989). This was a case of disguising a retreat, one that offended both the president and his supporters, with rhetoric and symbolic action. (One can argue that it may have been good short-run politics but hardly an effective way to educate the public about the realities of global politics.)

When the summit negotiations in Iceland broke down in October 1986, the immediate reaction was one of dismay. But after a week of polling, the White House staff was ready to put the president on television with a speech carefully crafted to punch the right buttons. The "shovel brigade" cleverly pictured the events not as a breakdown of strategic arms negotiations but as only a temporary near-miss for disarmament in which the president had hung tough and refused to give up his SDI for the sake of achieving an immediate agreement. Repeated surveys supported his position by about a three-to-one margin, and his popularity rating rose moderately (Americans Talk Security, 1987, p. 283).

Contemporary Soviet-American relations well illustrate an ambivalence of popular attitudes and policy preferences. For most of the cold war period, basic American attitudes toward the Soviet Union were highly negative; on a list of twenty-five or thirty countries toward which people could express their overall feelings, the USSR was always near the bottom. Figure 3.5 plots, on a "temperature" scale from +100 to −500, changes in popular attitudes toward the Soviet Union and China as recorded by American Institute of Public Opinion (AIPO) and National Opinion Research Center (NORC) national surveys. People are asked to rate a country on a scale of +5 "for something you like very much" to −5 "for something you dislike very much"; each of the scale positions is multiplied by the percentage of the population choosing that position, and then these are summed to produce the temperature rating for each survey. As the graph

Figure 3.5. Opinion toward China and the Soviet Union. Source: AIPO (Gallup) and National Opinion Research Center.

shows, attitudes toward the USSR improved slowly into the détente era (early 1970s), cooled (while those toward China continued to warm) under the impact of détente's decay and the anti-Soviet rhetoric of the early Reagan administration years, and then recovered by 1989 to almost a neutral level, higher even than during détente.[14] The new cautious neutrality was also apparent when the *New York Times* asked people whether they thought of the Soviet Union as an enemy, a friend, or neither. In 1985, 54 percent said enemy, 36 percent neither, and only 5 percent friend. By 1988 the equivalent numbers were 30 enemy, 33 neither, and 28 friend (Hinckley, 1990). It is hard to imagine a much more even spread.

As is well known, Soviet leader Mikhail Gorbachev's domestic policies and diplomatic efforts have gained him substantial worldwide popularity. His popularity rating rose in 1988 to a level higher than Ronald Reagan's in most of Europe and very nearly to Reagan's in the United States. Moreover, assessments were positive in every voter group in the American population. Attitudes toward the Soviet Union itself were more complex, reflecting both optimism and continued suspicion. The optimism showed in estimates of whether relations between the United States and the Soviet Union were getting better or worse. In 1986, 60 percent of the population said "staying the same" and only 24 percent "better"; by 1988 the situation had more than switched, to 68 percent saying "better" and only 24 percent "same," with just 5 percent "worse" (Americans Talk Security, July 1988, pp. 115, 54).

President Reagan once called the Soviet Union "an evil empire." In 1984, 56 percent of the population agreed with him in one survey and 55 percent in another. But by the end of 1987— even before the president himself said he no longer felt that way—the equivalent percentages in two surveys had fallen to 38

---

14. Attitudes toward China fell back less when détente cooled, and resumed improvement at a slower and steadier pace. No ratings since the imposition of martial law in June 1989 are available. The apparent volatility of attitudes toward China is exaggerated by changes in the label used to identify the country. In the 1967 survey it was referred to by the (for Americans) unfavorable label of "Communist China," and in 1972 and 1978 by the similarly unfavorable label of "Red China." In 1979, 1980, and 1983 it was "Mainland China/Communist China," and in other years simply the neutral "China." Unfavorable terms may lower the score about 50 points.

and 32 (*Los Angeles Times* press release, December 20, 1987;
Public Agenda, 1988). People also changed their assessment of
Soviet foreign policy goals. In 1984, they were asked whether
the Soviet Union was more interested in "maintaining peaceful
relations with the West" or in "achieving global domination";
58 percent of the population chose "domination." By 1988 only
38 percent said "domination," and 51 percent chose "maintaining peaceful relations" (Yankelovich and Harman, 1988).

As noted earlier in this chapter, this still does not mean that
Americans trust the Russians, particularly Russians other than
Gorbachev himself. Solid majorities in 1987 and 1988 believed
that the "Soviets are still supporting communist revolutions in
Central America" (83 percent), that they "are constantly testing,
probing for weakness, and take advantage whenever they find a
way" (71 percent), that it is "likely that the Soviets will increase
support of countries like Libya and terrorist groups in the Middle
East" (69 percent), and that it is "likely that the Soviets will
attack other nations the way they invaded Afghanistan" (66
percent). By the end of 1988 most (54 percent) no longer regarded
the Soviet Union as a serious or very serious threat to the United
States, but 45 percent still did (compared with 76 percent in
1985.) But people also said that Americans "should be thinking
of peaceful solutions as well as aggressive ones; picking a fight
with the Soviet Union is too dangerous in a nuclear world" (96
percent); and that "the U.S. and the Soviet Union must never
settle their differences by going to war" (85 percent). More than
80 percent agreed that "the Soviet Union and the U.S. share a
number of foreign policy interests such as prevention of war,
arms control, and stabilizing relations between them," and
almost as many concurred that Soviet external actions "often
stem from genuine fears for Russian security" (Holsti, 1988;
Public Agenda, 1988; Yankelovich and Harman, 1988; Americans Talk Security, January 1989, p. 58).

Here, then, is a version of the practical realism with which
we began this chapter. Americans now see the East-West conflict
as a continuing struggle for influence, one that will go on for a
long time. The adversary is powerful and will continue to probe
for advantages; Americans must be prepared to resist. Yet they
do not see the struggle as a Manichaean one, or as one that is
likely to be won or lost in any final sense. They will settle for

a *balance* of power in a realist's world. They see the greatest threat of "loss" as one where both sides suffer in an arms race or, worse, in a nuclear war. Hence most of them are ready to negotiate means to keep the peace and lower tensions. In this perception most Americans are neither hawks nor doves, but—in terms of the Harvard aviary—owls.

A major project (Public Agenda, 1988) presented Americans with four different images of the future, and through a series of surveys and discussion groups estimated the attractiveness of each. Each is characterized by a battery of statements too long to be repeated here, but we can get some of the flavor. One is labeled "U.S. gains the upper hand"; as suggested earlier, even as an ideal this attracts only a fairly small minority (24 percent) of the population. Another, the isolationist option to "defend only North America," was preferred by a mere 4 percent. The two leading choices were "eliminate the nuclear threat; compete otherwise," with 28 percent approval, and "cooperative problem solving," with 46 percent. The first of these is the more "realist," especially as it envisages drastic cuts in nuclear arsenals rather than their abolition; it anticipates some agreements to reduce the danger of escalation to nuclear war, but the continuation of vigorous competition, especially in the Third World. The vision of cooperative problem-solving is more nearly "idealist," with images of a nonadversarial relationship with the Soviet Union like the one the United States now enjoys with China, and cooperation on a wide range of common problems such as nuclear proliferation, AIDS, and terrorism. It is not a vision devoid of Soviet-American rivalry, but the rivalry is tempered by the need to collaborate against mutual threats to survival. Not all who prefer it really think it will be achieved; for many the jury on Soviet intentions remains out.

There *is* a touch of idealism in contemporary American attitudes, as perhaps there has always been. Despite their skepticism about Soviet intentions, most (57 percent) agree that "the differences between America and the Soviet Union are not that great and permanent peace is possible. Therefore, summit talks should be used mainly to produce real progress in arms control and other efforts to arrive a permanent peace." Perhaps this is putting too many words into people's mouths: "permanent peace" is a heady phrase, and one can agree with the earlier parts of the sentence without buying into the last words. Yet even in a 1986 survey in which 83 percent of Americans said they were suspicious rather than trusting of the Soviet Union, the reasons they gave were instructive: 11 percent cited Soviet nuclear military power, 27 percent cited communist ideology, and 45 percent the Soviets' "aggressive international behavior." In other words, Americans' suspicions of the Soviet Union are not necessarily written in stone; if the Soviets act "better," American attitudes may change accordingly (Hinckley, 1989). And at the time of writing, at least, the Soviets have been acting "better."

We will return in detail to the matter of Soviet-American relations in Chapter 5. But on that issue, as well as others, it is well to remember that public attitudes do change—they have in the past few years, and one can imagine conditions wherein they could change dramatically once again. Furthermore, democracy is hardly just a system of leaders listening to the vox populi and acting accordingly. Leaders do sometimes lead, and can change attitudes as well as respond to them. As we noted, different leaders labor under different popular expectations, and thus have different kinds of opportunities both to shape attitudes and to maneuver within the political space those attitudes delineate. Their skills in persuasion and "packaging" differ. So in the next chapter we turn to exploring the complex interaction between leaders and led.

4

Who Controls Whom?

The action of the mass depends on the quality of the choices presented.

Walter Lippmann, *Public Opinion*

There are four possible interpretations of the relationship between public opinion and national security policy. The first is that public opinion is *controlling*: that policy obeys the dictates of popular opinion, as stated in the extreme versions of democratic theory and mythology. This view is rejected by those whose basic premise is that the public is apathetic toward and largely indifferent to national security policy. Others acknowledge a degree of public interest and control, but based on vast ignorance, only sporadic interest, and volatile opinion; thus public control, to the degree it exists, will too often be pernicious. Public control thus may or may not be seen as strong, depending on assumptions about information and interest, and the normative judgment of any control is similarly dependent on such assumptions.

The view of public opinion as controlling is reversed by those who insist that public opinion is itself *controlled*: policymakers basically shape and manipulate opinion; the democratic mythology is false, and ruling elites persuade the populace to support whatever the leaders wish to do. They may succeed either because of inherent public ignorance and apathy or because the level of public information and the direction of public attitudes are sufficiently malleable.

A third view is that the two groups are mutually *irrelevant*: leaders do not obey public opinion, but neither do they control it—and they don't need to control it. Policy and opinion thus essentially go their separate ways.

Finally there is the view that opinion and policy *interact*: each influences the other, depending on the political and social context. This view does not exclude the possibility that either the public or the elite may be wrongheaded, but it does imply a certain degree of public interest, information, and "rationality."

Obviously the first three of these interpretations are extreme. Reality is that there is a bit of truth as well as exaggeration in each of them, leading us most closely but imperfectly to the fourth. We shall briefly review some evidence relevant to each interpretation, drawing on data and analyses about conflict and war, foreign policy, and public opinion in general. Previous analyses (e.g., Cohen, 1973; Hughes, 1978) simply do not point to a clear conclusion. We shall also deal with the special case of the relation between public opinion and legislators' behavior, and then with the degree of, and reasons for, changes in public opinion. We shall conclude with a discussion of the structure of belief systems, and make a key point missed by all existing theories: namely, that in a pluralistic system where opinion divides across several distinct dimensions, policymaking coalitions will be unstable even if public opinion is substantially unchanging.

Does the Public Really Care?

Some observers charge that the mass public is apathetic; whatever opinions it may express are grounded in ignorance and lack of sustained interest in foreign affairs. Most people's basic concerns are so far elsewhere that, to all intents and purposes, their "opinions" on foreign affairs can be, and are, properly dismissed as irrelevant. A substantial body of work does support part of this proposition (Caspary, 1970; Leigh, 1976), and a large literature reviews the concepts of issue publics, the attentive public, and the general public. The latest and most persuasive examination of the topic finds that only about 5 percent of the population—overlapping heavily though not exclusively with the upper echelon of educational, income, and occupational strata—can be considered politically active on *any* matter (not just foreign policy). The largest group—75 percent—constitutes a middle mass that moves in and out of politics, and 20 percent are apolitical. This delineation contrasts with earlier characterizations of about 20 percent of the population as an "attentive public" (Neuman, 1986).

Many observers contend that the situation is even worse for matters of foreign and security policy, about which people allegedly care little and know less. Information levels on foreign affairs frequently do seem low across the broad public. For example, in 1964, 42 percent of the population did not know that the United States was a member of NATO, and in 1985 only 36 percent were aware of the ABM treaty. Throughout the 1980s there was popular confusion about who was fighting on which side in Central America, with only a minority being able correctly to identify the Marxists in El Salvador and Nicaragua (Nincic, 1988b). Analysts who wish to minimize the role of popular participation in the formulation of security policy frequently cite these and similar data; for example, that in early 1979 only 34 percent of the American population could correctly identify the two countries involved in the SALT negotiations.

Even these indications of widespread ignorance, however, can be deceptive, confusing active recall of information with somewhat more latent recognition. For instance, when respondents were given a list of possible purposes of SALT, 58 percent correctly answered that the talks concerned long-range weapons. Actual knowledge levels are higher than they appear from quiz-show questioning. And the proportion of Americans who could define the concept "NATO" (34 percent; 29 percent of the British public) is similar to the proportion who could define "welfare state" and "electoral college" (Neuman, 1986, p. 17; Sabin, 1986, p. 143; Plous, 1988). Furthermore, there are some intriguing patterns in popular knowledge, including that the level of awareness and detailed information on nuclear *weapons* is twice as high as awareness and information on *arms control* agreements and negotiations (Graham, 1988). This fact probably says more about patterns of attention in the mass media than about inherent popular ignorance.

Admittedly, popular interest in such matters is usually not as high as the level of interest in all domestic political problems combined. This is especially true in the large and relatively insulated United States. But interest in international affairs has been high during what most observers would, in retrospect, acknowledge as key periods in the consolidation or change of

American foreign policy. Low levels of detailed information should not be confused with lack of interest.

New research demonstrates that foreign policy issues were salient to the public, and influential to voting, in most post–World War II elections. Furthermore, an increase in the public's approval of the president's handling of foreign policy is linked— like its approval of his economic policy, though somewhat less closely—to its general approval of the president's performance in office. In turn, individuals who approve his general performance are very likely to vote for him. There is some question here about the degree to which approval of policy causes voting decisions (as opposed to a halo effect of approval of policies following a decision to support a candidate) but nonetheless this suggests that agreement with a presidential candidate's position on foreign policy significantly matters to election outcomes (Aldrich, et al., 1989; Nincic and Hinckley, 1990). Even with low levels of information, people often vote "rationally" through indicating their understanding and opinion of the political system's past performance (Fiorina, 1981).

As Figure 4.1 shows, concern with foreign affairs and security policy as the country's "most important problem" was very high

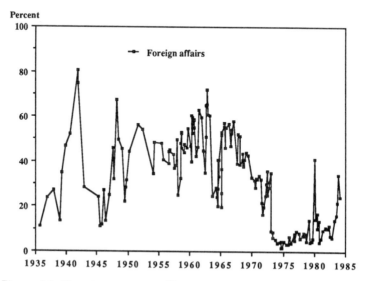

Figure 4.1. Most important problem: percentage answering "foreign affairs" Source: Data from Smith, 1985.

during the early years of the cold war, first as the shape of Soviet-American rivalry emerged and then during the Korean War. It dropped sharply in 1963 after the Cuban missile crisis. (Arguably the "lesson" of that crisis to most people was not that war continued as an imminent threat, but rather that American strength had forced the Soviets to back down and thus that the United States could effectively keep the peace.) It rose again shortly thereafter, as American forces became involved in the Vietnam war, and stayed high until the troops began to come home and the era of détente set in. A new peak appeared in January 1980 in response to events in Iran and Afghanistan (with smaller peaks of 38 percent in January 1974 and 31 percent in May 1979 if one were to count the ambiguous "energy" category as foreign). It rose again in 1983, staying moderately high through a period that included a number of dramatic and threatening international events, including the engagement of American troops in Lebanon and Grenada, the shooting down of the Korean airliner, and some subsequent dramatic acts of international terrorism and counterterrorism (such as the bombing of Libya; see Smith, 1985; *Gallup Report*, September 1986). Arguably, Americans have been interested in foreign policy when it showed the greatest potential for affecting them, and have sensibly turned their major interest to other matters (recessions, civil rights in the 1960s, and so on) whose impact on their well-being was greater during periods of relative international quiet.

Those who lament the low levels of public information often forget that intensity of opinion is highly correlated with extreme preferences on a policy spectrum, and that intensity of opinion also is often associated with high levels of information. People inform themselves about what they *care* about—but not necessarily with "knowledge" in the sense of cognitive complexity. The extremist is often the one with simple judgments and uncomplicated solutions. An advocate of democracy therefore would not *necessarily* want a highly informed public on matters of security policy if that would mean a public with intense and "extreme" opinions. The advocate would want the information to be available, but not necessarily want everyone to seek it intensely (Sartori, 1987, ch. 5).

Arguments about public ignorance and apathy thus constitute only partial truths which may help to build the egos of college professors and professional politicians. But even presidents sometimes show their ignorance: remember the reaction of the media to Gerald Ford's amnesia about the communist government of Poland, or Ronald Reagan's many famous bloopers, such as his impression, as commander-in-chief, that intercontinental missiles could be recalled after launching. The appropriate standard against which to judge the level of public knowledge is not necessarily obvious, and one should beware of self-serving elitist urgings to keep responsibility in the hands of those who know the facts and therefore know best.

Is Public Opinion Fickle?

Next is the matter of whether public opinion frequently flip-flops on major issues. Some observers feared, especially in the early cold war years, that mass opinion was highly volatile, with whims changing in response to every contradictory international event. If public opinion on vital issues of national security were very unstable it would not provide a reliable basis for public policy. One would hardly want policymakers to be very responsive to such shifting opinion.

These fears have proved groundless. Almond's (1950) "mood theory" of volatility was effectively challenged by Caspary (1970). It was essentially destroyed by Shapiro and Page (1988), who cogently posited that opinion stability is the rule and that when change does occur it happens in logical patterns in relation to world circumstances. They examined more than four hundred foreign policy items that had been repeated in national surveys at various times over a fifty-year period. They found that slightly over half of those items showed no statistically significant change in opinion at all, that half of those which did change showed shifts of fewer than 10 percentage points, and that there was very little fluctuation in the direction of change in opinions about foreign policy. Foreign policy items, and particularly war-related items, did, however, show more rapid *rates* of change than did domestic policy items. The authors regard these as appropriate changes in response to rapid alternations in the international environment as interpreted by the American media and political leadership. Thus American citizens "have formed and changed their policy preferences in a rational fashion—in a manner worthy of serious consideration in deliberation about the direction and content of U.S. foreign policy."

Although large-scale swings in public opinion and security policy did occur in the early post–World War II years, opinion on major issues stabilized by the early 1950s. Neither the early volatility nor the stabilization should be surprising, since it took most of the decade after 1945 to resolve vigorous intra-elite debates over issues like the nature of the Soviet Union, isolationism versus internationalism, containment-rollback, and the relative efficacy of military versus economic and diplomatic implements of policy. Thereafter, opinions changed little until major policy events had their impact. Opinions on major foreign policy issues usually are more stable than are attitudes toward individual leaders—recall the volatility of presidents' approval ratings. Moreover, different issues are important to different "issue publics" of informed, interested, and politically active citizens (Converse, 1964); even within the general area of foreign policy there are distinctive audiences and players for, for example, arms control, Arab-Israeli relations, and Central America. The attitudes of such issue publics—the elements of the public which matter most—are likely to be more stable than those of the public in general. Mass volatility is thus not properly to be feared.

Some time ago Deutsch and Merritt (1965; also Brody and Page, 1975) established, for the United States and several European countries, that sustained change in basic attitudes resulted only from repeated, dramatic events. Later study of attitudes in four European democracies found similar results. Sentiment toward foreign countries was generally stable and consistent with measures of cooperation and conflict with those countries; short-run changes in policy sometimes were reflected in attitude changes, but the relationship usually was not strong (Abravanel and Hughes, 1975). Attitudes can remain stable over long periods of time even when one might think change should take place. For example, American opinions concerning the feasibility and desirability of building defensive strategic systems (either the ABM or SDI) have been remarkably stable over a forty-year period (Graham, 1986). In Israel, a very dramatic shift in attitudes occurred in response to Sadat's peace initiative and visit to Jerusalem. The percentage of Israelis believing that "Egypt is really interested in realizing a peace agreement with us on conditions that can be accepted" rose to about 90 from a previous 57, and those who said they expected no more war with Arab countries jumped from a previously stable 10–15 percent to about 50. Both of these, however, dropped back almost to their previous levels within six months (Guttman, 1978; Stone, 1982, pp. 31–35).

The rally 'round the flag effect might plausibly be cited as evidence for the proposition that in the short run, and at least on foreign policy issues, public opinion is volatile and readily manipulated by the government. But its effect can readily be exaggerated. Remember that typically only about 5 percent of the population shifts to view the president more favorably. In addition, the effect is truly ephemeral, with a half-life of no more than a month or two (Mueller, 1973; Lee, 1977; Kernell, 1978; Benson, 1982; Brody, 1984). The effect is so short that a president who wants to live by it must continually be creating new crises—which is a conceivable but risky policy. Furthermore, use of foreign policy crises for generating support can readily backfire; if the crisis is long unresolved the president's approval rating is likely to end up worse than at the beginning. And perhaps most important, not just any president can succeed in building support with just any foreign policy action; public expectations of different presidents, and the policies they are trusted to pursue, vary substantially. All this was discussed at length in the preceding chapters.

These findings basically refer to the stability of opinion at the aggregate level; that is, the proportion of the population holding a given opinion is relatively stable. They do not tell us about the stability of individuals' opinions: if half the people changed their minds in opposite directions the aggregates would not change. In that sense, even if individuals' opinions were as shallow as some theorists imagine, and people did change their minds frequently, the overall balance of opinion might be stable and therefore predictable to policymakers. Individual attitude changes thus might not matter much for analyzing the consequences for the political system; politicians care less about shifts among individuals than about changes in the overall proportion of votes that may be cast for them.

It is possible to distinguish between aggregate and individual stability only with a research design that repeatedly tracks the opinion of particular individuals. That procedure, known as a panel design, is very expensive, and rarely done. Nevertheless, in those cases where it has been tried for foreign policy issues, the stability of attitudes over time has proven very high. On the basic organizing principles of foreign policy, people do not change their minds readily (Achen, 1975; Erikson, 1978b, 1979). A panel study of people's presidential performance ratings also found that those ratings were relatively stable over a period of several months (the best predictor of the most recent rating was the individual's previous rating). When they did change the changes were in response to changes in the economic and international environment, mediated by patterns of attention and the individual's partisan allegiances; in other words, certainly not frivolous changes (Ostrom and Simon, 1988).

How Are Opinion Change and Policy Change Related?

The view that public opinion is thoroughly controlled by the elites is as misleading as the opposite and simpleminded one that "the people" always have their way. The first has a long and honorable tradition in radical thought, in which the elites are said to shape the dominant political culture in a way that provides the masses with a "false consciousness" as to their true interests. In consequence they come to accept the dominant values of capitalism and, in foreign policy, of militant anticommunism. The dominant myth of the society serves to reinforce the interests of the ruling classes, and the key elements of that myth are beyond the bounds of question in politically respectable discourse.

The most subtle form of this analysis is expressed in the line of thought, from Antonio Gramsci, about "cultural hegemony." In that understanding, the dominant culture is primarily the creature of the ruling classes, and serves instead of overt repressive force, in "democratic" political systems, as a persuasive means to prevent challenge to the rulers' interests. The arguments about cultural hegemony are complex, and in many respects defy systematic empirical confirmation or disconfirmation. Discussions about the long-term autonomy and role of popular preferences are not appropriately dealt with here. The concept, moreover, is of a dynamic phenomenon, one that owes its power to its ability to incorporate important elements from the subordinate cultures.[1] As such it is not a pure expression of the view that "public opinion" is utterly passive and manipulated.

Anyone can readily think of some issues on which even stable mass opinion and policy have pointed in opposite directions for a long time, issues on which the majority of the population has not been able to translate its preferences into public policy through the democratic process, at least without long delay. As we noted in Chapter 3, elite consensus in Western Europe has managed to sustain certain national security policies despite substantial mass sentiment for modification of those policies, of which the clearest example is the matter of no first use of nuclear weapons. Majorities in ten European countries have long favored a policy of no first use. Yet their governments have refused to countenance the idea on the grounds that it might comprise dangerous policy, and might fail because of a public unwillingness to pay the economic price that a nonnuclear defense of Western Europe would entail.

In maintaining their policies, however, the governments have not so obviously overridden popular preferences. We noted the degree of popular ambivalence on these matters, including an "existential" willingness to keep the weapons in a deterrent posture that could lead to first use, and a reluctance to take *unilateral* actions or declarations of no first use. As a result, it is simplistic, and erroneous, to say that the governments have been acting in violation of any clear popular directive. Such instances certainly do not prove that public opinion is "irrelevant" in any general sense, but they do weaken the argument that the public always gets its way in any immediate or direct manner. The no-first-use issue well illustrates how popular sentiments bracket a range of policies within which governments can choose; it does not necessarily show that the populace is either muddle-headed or ignored.

An example of how ambiguous and complex a phenomenon this can be is the ratification of the Panama Canal treaties under

---

1. For American readers the classic version may well be Mills, 1956; a good introduction to Gramscian ideas is Lear, 1985, and for a rather sympathetic liberal rendition see Lindblom, 1977.

the Carter administration. Public opinion consistently opposed ratification; Carter urged senators nevertheless to "do the states-manlike thing" in the national interest. Ultimately he got his two-thirds majority, with the polls still against him. But he was helped in the end by the interpretation—a mistaken one, as it turned out—that observers put on the late polls. They thought they saw an opinion shift in favor of the treaties, and several senators used that shift as a reason, or a cover, for voting aye. Was this an example of popular sovereignty, or at least of defer-ence to the *apparent* popular will (Smith and Hogan, 1987)?

On the matter of whether legislators—representatives in Con-gress or in national parliaments—are attentive to public opinion, we may ask first whether they respond primarily (if at all) to conditions in their own constituencies. As representatives of limited geographical areas, legislators are presumably closer to the vox populi and hence in a position to be more responsive than is an executive who must carry out policy in the name of the entire nation. There is some systematic evidence specifically on matters of war and peace, and more on general relationships between voters' attitudes, by constituency, and those of their representatives on a range of issues including foreign policy.

The classic study by Miller and Stokes (1966) found that con-stituents' foreign policy attitudes seemed to have little impact on members of Congress. The relation between legislators' vot-ing records on foreign policy and the attitudes of their consti-tuencies (as assessed by survey research) was very weak, and even weaker was that between legislators' voting and their per-ceptions of their constituents' views on foreign policy. This study has been subjected to many attempts to reproduce or refine its conclusions, with mixed results. In Sweden, voters and leg-islators' opinions were similar on defense policy but not on more general matters of foreign policy (Goldmann et al., 1986). Erikson (1978a) found a discernible, though still weak, relation between constituency opinion and both representatives' attitudes and roll call voting on foreign policy. Page et al. (1984) reported a some-what stronger relation between constituents' survey responses and congressional roll call voting, but had no foreign policy issues in their sample. In Miller's earlier study (1964), represen-tatives from closely contested districts, whether Republicans or Democrats, tended to vote very much alike, suggesting that electoral competitition tends to make representatives more responsive to constituency opinion. Achen (1978), however, reported that winners of contested elections were no more representative of their constituents' opinions than were losers, on all issues or on foreign policy issues in particular.

The conclusion seems to be that the idealized (but not Burkean) vision of constituency representation is but distantly approached, especially on foreign policy issues. Perhaps this is not surprising in an era of weak local party organizations and nationally organized campaigns and fund-raising. It also is not surprising in an era when 96 percent of congressional representatives who seek relection are in fact returned to office. An incumbent, knowing the likelihood that he or she will be reelected anyway, is not under enormous pressure to conform to constitutency views on particular issues.

On long-term matters of change in opinion and/or policy, however, attitudes toward military spending are consistent with a model of "normal" opinion stability and rational attitude change in relation to events. Opinions proved fairly stable through most of the 1950s and 1960s, with about a quarter of the population wanting to spend more on defense, about a fifth wishing to spend less, and the rest expressing no desire for a change. Attitudes did shift thereafter, as did national and international conditions. The cumulative impact of the Vietnam war produced an aversion to things military, so that by the beginning of the 1970s only a fifth of the population wanted to spend more on defense—and half the population wanted to spend less. Some observers (Allison, 1970–71; Russett, 1974) thought this represented a semipermanent change, but they were wrong. By the beginning of the Reagan era, the portion of the population wanting to spend more on defense rose above 40 percent (and briefly to 60), and then fell again to a level even lower than that of the Vietnam era. In effect, the desire for a strong defense grew again during a period when American military budgets continued to drop as a fraction of GNP while Soviet acquisition of strategic weapons proceeded apace, détente faded, the Russians invaded Afghanistan, and the Iranians humiliated the United States (Free and Watts, 1980; Gergen, 1980; Russett and DeLuca, 1981). But then, as the Reagan military budget soared, opinion shifted once more toward the conclusion that the defense buildup had gone too far and in a new era it was time to emphasize other priorities.

Opinion changes certainly occurred, but they were neither sudden nor frequent, and seemed to be responding reasonably to changes in the world. Overall, as Figure 4.2 suggests, preferences for change in military expenditures (survey percentages saying military spending was "too much" are graphed to the scale on the right) corresponded fairly closely to changes in actual military spending in constant 1987 dollars (graphed to the scale on the left). The post-Vietnam antimilitary feeling and the military spending cuts are evident, as is the desire in the late Carter and early Reagan years for increases. The Reagan administration satisfied the initial wish for military increases, but resisted the subsequent public sentiment that military spending had become excessive.

Analysis of the data suggests that decisions about military spending usually *respond* to public opinion. In a previous analysis I examined relationships that assumed both simultaneous change and lagged relationships in both directions (that is, opinion leading spending changes and vice versa), and found that the strongest relationship was one between opinion in one year and

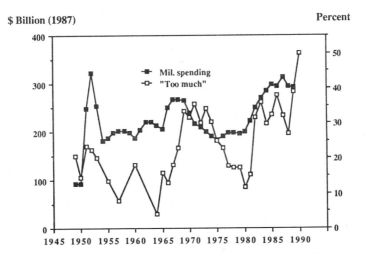

Figure 4.2. Public support for increased military spending, and actual military spending in 1987 dollars. Source: Data compiled by Thomas Hartley for the Yale project on public opinion and national security.

changes in actual military spending in the subsequent year. That is, the larger the proportion of the population that wanted to reduce military spending, the greater the actual percentage reduction in the next year (Russett, 1989).[2] Other comprehensive studies of the interaction between attitudes toward defense spending and congressional decisions to increase or cut the president's military spending proposals have also found a strong relation between public opinion and subsequent congressional policy (Jacobson, 1985; Ostrom and Marra, 1986). Together, this evidence tends to support the proposition that on this issue at least the government does in some sense respond to the voice of the people. Public opinion did change, and was in some sense "unstable"—but in its changes it operated as a stabilizing force on actual military spending.

President Nixon's policy of gradual withdrawal of American troops and "Vietnamization" of the war was in effect imposed on the president by public opinion as the price of domestic tranquillity and any support for continuing the war. The mechanism for enforcing public pressure worked through Congress, with congressional elections changing bodies by replacing pro-war representatives with antiwar freshman ones, and changing the minds of continuing representatives in part by the threat of electoral defeat if they did not shift their positions (Kissinger, 1979; A. Katz, 1988). This period coincided with an ongoing breakdown of the seniority system and leadership controls in Congress, enhancing the power of rank-and-file members.

For long-term public opinion and government policy changes on many issues in the United States, the best systematic empirical evidence is provided by Page and Shapiro (1983). They found that, in foreign policy as well as other issues, the government was more likely to change in response to a shift in public opinion than vice versa, and to shift in the direction preferred by the public. An earlier study also found that in nearly 250 cases public preferences in the polls for or against change in policy were generally consistent with subsequent federal government actions, and that this was especially true of foreign policy issues (Monroe, 1979). Even so, there were many exceptions to these

---

2. Adjusted $r^2 = .55$; $p = .001$; autocorrelation is not, by the standard tests, a problem.

general findings. Moreover, it is possible that policymakers might first form a new opinion, then persuade opinion leaders in the media who in turn persuade the mass public so that finally the very people in government who initiated the change can "respond" to public opinion.

One example which suggests that the causal direction often runs from national policy and international events to opinion is public attitudes toward China and the Soviet Union. (Shown at the end of Chapter 3, in Figure 3.5). They appear to constitute a case in which attitude changes generally follow major policy shifts, but once set do not vary greatly in response to short-term ups and downs of policy. Not surprisingly, popular images of friends and adversaries depend on the general direction of foreign policy, including shifts in international alignment from enemy to ally.

Mass attitudes of course respond not only, or even primarily, to "objective" international conditions, but to how those conditions are interpreted by the elites and the mass media. The standard wisdom has long been that, especially on issues of foreign and security policy, there is a two-step flow of communications, first from the policymakers and the mass media to opinion leaders in communities, and then to the mass public. Similar views postulate movement downward from the "top-dogs" or center to the "underdogs" or periphery (Katz and Lazars-feld, 1955; Galtung, 1967).

Recent work, however, suggests that the process is more stratified, and that those who regularly follow politics in the mass media talk primarily to one another other and not to those who have a low level of political information and interest; political discussion is thus stratified and the trickle-down effect is weak (Neuman, 1986, p. 147). Research on opinion about issues such as defense spending, the presence of American troups in Lebanon, and aid to the Nicaraguan contras indicates that the content of the electronic media is an excellent predictor of opinion within a very short time-frame. Indeed, the lag between media message and opinion response may well be less than a day, and the effect no longer discernible after a week. Such a very short response time suggests little time for a two-stage process of discussion and dissemination; at least in the television era, the media effect seems direct (Fan, 1988).

If so, more attention needs to be given to this direct influence of the media on mass opinion in the domains of foreign and security policy, domains which are often remote to most citizens. Because of their remoteness and character of symbolic politics, they are events to be interpreted for people by the media. Public opinion seems to respond to the views of prominent television commentators, and to testimony by ostensibly non-partisan experts as reported on television. It also responds to the media efforts of popular presidents, but not to the efforts of presidents scoring below 50 percent on the presidential job performance poll ratings (Page et al., 1987). However, "even *intensive efforts over several months by highly popular presidents* appear to bring about changes in opinion poll results of only some 5 or 10 percentage points, hardly a tidal wave" (Page and Shapiro, 1984, p. 659, my emphasis).

Changes of that magnitude may be very important in determining the outcomes of close elections. Furthermore, there are exceptional cases when the right kind of dramatic event and an intensive media strategy are combined, producing a much more striking short-term change in public opinion. Perhaps the strongest example is the 25-point shift in public opinion that apparently resulted from President Reagan's speech on the invasion of Grenada. Even so, overall these findings reinforce the earlier evidence for stability rather than volatility of opinion. The media can shape the form of attitude change and influence its magnitude—on the margins—but the media alone cannot initiate significant change in attitudes (Iyengar and Kinder, 1987; Munton, 1984).

Insofar as change does occur, it results from differences in individuals' exposure to the media, the credibility of particular leaders or media figures with different individuals, individuals' level of information and interest in policy, and the social network of individuals' direct contacts with policymaking. Such a list of influences sounds rather like an epidemiological model of the determinants of a disease within a population. Individuals are differently exposed by their placement in social networks, and are differently susceptible or immune on ideological or personality grounds when exposed. As highly susceptible persons become exposed, the disease may spread at exponential rates;

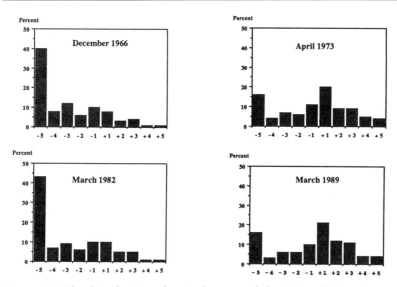

Figure 4.3. The distribution of attitudes toward the Soviet Union. Source: AIPO (Gallup) and National Opinion Research Council National Surveys.

later, as the most vulnerable and exposed have already contracted it, the rate of spread decreases, and large segments of the population may be spared. The distribution of likelihood of contracting the disease may be bimodal; a large portion of the population highly vulnerable, and another large portion only minimally so.[3]

Something like this may be seen in popular attitudes toward China and the Soviet Union. Instead of the summary temperature score for each survey, Figures 4.3 and 4.4 show the distribution of attitudes across the population at various times. In the 1960s the vast majority of the population held very negative views of both countries, with the distribution highly skewed toward a single mode at the far left-hand side. But in the 1970s a second mode (or peak) formed at the +1 point on the scale; in 1973 as much as 47 percent of the population rated the Soviet Union somewhere on the positive side, as did 47 percent of the population for China. By the early 1980s attitudes toward the Soviet Union had chilled, returning to almost the same pattern

3. Good mathematical models exist for this in attitude research as well; e.g., Abelson, 1964. A useful if dated review of diffusion processes is Katz, Levin, and Hamilton, 1963.

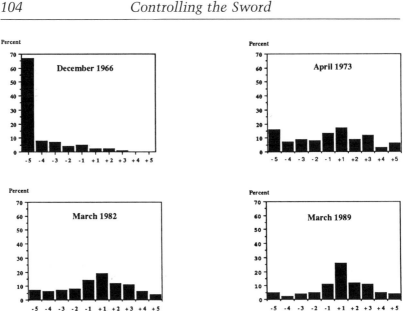

Figure 4.4. The distribution of attitudes toward China. Source: Same as Figure 4.3.

as in 1966. Those toward China, however, continued to warm, becoming unimodal once more—but with the mode at +1, and 66 percent of the population on the positive side (27 negative, 7 percent no opinion). Opinion and policy toward China achieved remarkable agreement, with sometimes one leading, sometimes the other (Kusnitz, 1984). Agreement of opinion and policy has also applied toward the Soviet Union. Toward that country, however, the "disease" of more positive attitudes was contained as American official policy and rhetoric shifted; the positive mode nearly vanished until the end of the 1980s, when it reappeared and the distribution of attitudes recovered about the same shape as in 1973.

Attitudes toward the Soviet Union and China have always been more positive among those with relatively high education and socioeconomic status, but the status differences were most marked in the early détente period of shift. When the opinion shift of the 1970s occurred, it was concentrated among those more educated, of higher social status, and presumably more interested in and informed about foreign affairs. Led by changes in national policy, these people adopted a slightly positive evaluation of these countries. By contrast, research into attitude change on the Vietnam war concluded that people who first opposed the war were relatively low in socioeconomic status and education (Hahn, 1970; Lunch and Sperlich, 1979; Bryen, 1980). The grassroots turned against the war before the Tet offensive, whereas the elite—which closely follows the media—changed its opinion only after the visually dramatic events of Tet. With both parts of the public then moving in the same direction, for different reasons, the administration had to respond (Moyers, 1968). If attitudes change at different rates throughout the population and the general public is not dependent on elites for its attitudes, this has important implications for the relationship between public opinion and policy.

The frequent emergence of bimodal distributions indicates important polarizations in mass communication networks; people tune in largely to opinions with which they already agree. The opinions people express will change only if people perceive that the general climate of opinion makes their own revised opinions acceptable. Noelle-Neumann (1984) uses the term "public opinion" to refer to that set of controversial opinions which an individual can express without feeling isolated. If people feel their opinions are not socially acceptable, they will not express them and, in a "spiral of silence," will make it less likely that others will be willing to express those same opinions.

Two further points with interesting implications for democratic theory can be made about individual information levels and opinion change. One is that the approved (Bayesian) method of decisionmaking is indeed constantly to revise one's opinion as further information becomes available. For example, I may start with the observation that the weather is highly unpredictable from day to day, and that it has rained about every other day for the last month. If so, I will at first estimate the chances of rain tomorrow as fifty-fifty. If I listen to the weather forecast this evening and it says clear, then presumably I should raise my own estimate of the chances of sunshine. But if I look out the window in the morning and see a dark sky, I probably should instead raise my estimate about the chances of rain to well over fifty-fifty. My opinion about the weather will have changed repeatedly as I have gathered new information. But at each point my opinion will have been based on the best information available to me, and my last opinion will be the best informed. Individuals may change their opinions often, and even dramatically, without being shallow or ignorant in doing so.

The second point is that even if a particular person has only a slightly better than fifty-fifty chance of being correct on a matter of factual information or having the opinion that will produce the "right" political results, the chances that the population aggregate will be right, deciding on a principle of majority rule, are immensely higher. Simple probability calculations show that if each individual has a 55 percent chance of expressing the "right" opinion and makes up his or her mind independently, the chances are almost 99.9 percent that a population of 1000 or more people will by majority decision choose the right one. In other words, the "wisdom" of the people as a whole may well exceed that of the individuals.[4]

The evidence suggests substantial public ability to form discriminating and stable opinions. Changes—on defense spending, attitudes toward adversaries, and tolerance for war, for example, do occur, but not precipitously and in a rather rational, informed manner. People do not change their opinions frivolously, nor are they easily led. Many writers have contended that popular opinion is manipulated by media and opinion elites. Some even allege that it is easier to manipulate opinion in democracies—despite the greater range of opinion that can be expressed openly—than in authoritarian societies, because in the latter the level of skepticism is already great and people are psychologically prepared for manipulation by the government (Jensen, 1982, cited in Arian et al., 1988). But when the basic content of opinion is reasonably stable over time—when neither mass nor elite opinion changes much—there is little basis to say that either is causally dominant. Under those circumstances, which often prevail, the policymakers' problem becomes more one of finding what actions will be acceptable within the existing range of opinion than of dramatically transforming opinion in the direction they prefer.

4. Nicholas Caritat de Condorcet in 1785 (cited in Page and Shapiro, forthcoming, ch. 1) reached a similar result with his jury principle.

Some Illustrations from the Policy World

Leaders in a real sense interact with public opinion, both responding to it and manipulating it. The chief of state who sees his popularity rating going down knows that he has to do something; when he does he may be said to be responding to public opinion. But if, for example, he responds to a recession-induced decline in popularity by using military force in order to invoke the rally 'round the flag effect, he surely is manipulating opinion in the sense that he is increasing his popularity without correcting the underlying causes of mass discontent that endangered his popularity in the first place. The irony is that decisions to use force are in principle among the most tightly held and least "democratic" decision processes. If the interaction we observe is democratic responsiveness, it is perverse, and "the people" are only partially to blame.

Successful leaders work with and around public opinion in tactical ways. In the modern era, Franklin Roosevelt retained Hadley Cantril to poll for him throughout the prewar and wartime years. He closely watched public opinion before Pearl Harbor, not to determine his basic policy, but to choose his tactics to move the United States toward support of Britain and ultimately into the war. First he chose greater military spending and lend-lease—not the draft or direct intervention—because these instruments offered the greatest potential for domestic approval (Cantril, 1967; Steele, 1978; Graham, 1989a). Near the end of World War II the Office of Public Affairs was organized in the State Department, to conduct both polls and "public education" of opinion leaders (Paterson, 1988, pp. 82–83).

John Kennedy had an aide assigned to poll-watching; Kennedy was the first to recognize the growing importance of television news, and shifted his schedule of personal interviews away from newspaper columnists to television commentators (Kern et al., 1983, p. 140). Lyndon Johnson was famous for carrying the latest survey reports in his pockets and waving them at visitors. Richard Nixon closely watched the polls on attitudes toward the Vietnam war. James Fallows said of his experience in the Carter administration, "The polling data I usually saw in the government were connected with the *salesmanship* of a program as opposed to the development of a policy . . . Polling data are useful to the extent that they tell you *how* to do things you have already decided to do for other reasons" (Cantril, 1980, p. 134; his emphasis).

Ronald Reagan and his staff brought the art form to a new height; their efforts vividly illustrate both how intense the activity of keeping track of public opinion may be and how hard it may be to say straightforwardly who is controlling whom. They established a sophisticated public opinion survey operation in the White House. Richard Wirthlin, the White House pollster, discussed his material with the president twenty-five times during his the first twenty-nine months in office (Beal and Hinckley, 1984). Every day the staff worried about how statements made at 9:00 A.M. would be received, how the statements would play with reporters at the noon press conferences, and then how they would be treated on the 6:00 P.M. television news. According to David Stockman, "For Mike Deaver and the others in the Reagan White House, reality happened once a day on the evening news. They lived off the tube" (quoted in Rose, 1988, p. 117). At one point in Reagan's second term, Deaver and Nancy Reagan reportedly used polls showing Americans' waning enthusiasm for defense spending to persuade the president to reduce his proposed military budget.

The U.S. Information Agency had long commissioned surveys in other countries, and officials there and in the State Department tracked the results. Information garnered was used in designing speeches by American officials to foreign audiences (Robinson and Meadow, 1982, p. 34). The innovation by the Reagan administration was how extensively it used survey research on attitudes about foreign affairs in its dealings with the American public. A Public Affairs Committee, chaired by an assistant to the president for communications and the deputy assistant to the president for national security affairs, was responsible for planning and coordinating domestic public affairs activities associated with national security. The committee's game with public opinion was an interactive one. "Public diplomacy" officials were commissioned to "see what turns Americans against the Sandinistas," and to use that material in speeches and news releases (Parry and Kornbluh, 1988; Hinckley, 1988a).

Administration pollsters used the surveys to target particular groups, identified demographically, politically, or ideologically so as to build and maintain a winning coalition, and aimed particular actions, speeches, and television spots at different groups (a sales operation not unlike, for instance, producing television spots aimed at selling detergent to southern working-class housewives). The composition of the coalition varied over time and from issue to issue even within the domain of foreign policy; for example, the supporters of aid to Afghanistan were not always the same who supported aid to the Nicaraguan contras.

Polls were especially relevant to the timing and shaping of the air strike against Libya. In 1986 a series of private polls were commissioned and reported to the crisis management center at the National Security Council. Between January and March they showed an increase from 49 to 66 in the percentage of Americans who said they were ready to support a military strike against a state that supported terrorism; in association with the administration's intensive public relations effort against Muhamar Gaddafi, Libya replaced Iran as the preferred target. But it had to be a limited and "reluctant" act. The American bombing raid took place on April 14. In one sense, the American people got just what they wanted; an affirmation of democratic theory. In another, the administration got what it wanted: a politically popular use of force against someone, and against its preferred target (Libya) rather than Iran or Syria, with which the U.S. government was negotiating (Anderson, 1988; Hinckley, 1988a).

Can anyone thoroughly separate the chicken from the egg? The three initial views identified in this chapter are wrong. Clearly public opinion and policymaking interact, sometimes with one leading and sometimes the other, with policymaking shaped in anticipation of public reaction and framed so as to make that reaction most favorable. "Anticipated reactions" do not deny the power of those whose reactions are anticipated. The rally effect and even its manipulation are in that sense expressions of popular power. Power is exercised less through mechanisms of active, participatory, rational voting than through acquiescence or rejection of policy and values. "Governments must pursue policies that maintain the support of voters, or at least do not provoke their disapproval. But in turn, voters, by their acquiescence, become responsible for the policies of government" (Natchez, 1985, p. 231).

Public opinion sets broad limits of constraint, identifying a range of policies within which decisionmakers can choose, and within which they must choose if they are not to face rejection in the voting booths. Its effect is likely to vary by issue, and by time-frame. In an immediate crisis initiated by a foreign power the direct input of public opinion may be small, although the incentives to get public approval still will be great and the anticipation of long-term public reaction will help shape the kind of action taken to meet the crisis. A major instrument of popular influence in the United States may often operate through congressional readings of public opinion and then through legislators' influence on the executive. Public opinion may be more effective as elections draw near. In an era of "permanent plebiscite" conducted by polls and electronic media, however, the interaction of public opinion and exercises of political drama by governmental leaders is a continuing phenomenon.

The Structure and Stability of Belief Systems

The notion of separated networks of opinion transmission, discussed above, also helps explain the phenomenon of consistency or structure of attitudes across several issues. Both elites and mass show evidence of this structure. Structured and somehow internally consistent attitudes are not likely to be volatile. Converse (1964) argued that belief systems, in general, would be more structured among the elites than among the mass for reasons that included logical, psychological, and social sources of constraint as well as lower levels of information in the mass public. Converse's findings have been subject to sharp challenge. The most recent evaluation (Achen, 1983) declares that Converse's work suffered from methodological flaws and that his conclusion was exaggerated—yet probably basically correct. Elites are, for example, more likely to take a differentiated view of which countries the United States should assist militarily if they were invaded; members of the general public are more likely to give the same answer—yes or no—for all countries (Reilly, 1983, p. 31).

Structure and consistency of attitude may be derived from cognitive processes of logic or psycho-logic. Structure may also result from differences in how important various issues are for different individuals, coupled with varying intensities of communication. For example, if we had what appeared to be a single dimension of foreign and domestic policy attitudes—with one end comprising people who are both hawks and domestic conservatives, and the other those who are both doves and domestic liberals—it might be because those who care about foreign policy and are hawks are largely in the same social networks with those who care primarily about domestic policy and are conservatives. If so, those for whom foreign policy is most salient and who are hawks are likely to persuade those domestic conservatives who don't care much about foreign policy to be hawks also; similarly the people who are oriented toward foreign policy are likely to adopt the views on domestic policy of those they talk to regularly who are more interested than they are in domestic policy. The patterns of social communication, more than a deliberate effort to achieve cognitive consistency, would thus account for what "consistency" appeared (Abelson, 1979).

This phenomenon fits with the conclusion noted above that most people have fairly low levels of knowledge on issues of security policy. They "tune in" to issues in a rational fashion, and depend on trusted social contacts or communications media to provide an orientation on issues to which they do not normally give much serious thought. "A paucity of information does not impede structure and consistency; on the contrary, it motivates the development and employment of structure" to make sense out of otherwise confusing bits of information (Hurwitz and Peffley, 1987, p. 1114; Sniderman and Tetlock, 1986).

The notion of structure in belief systems is often used to imply a single underlying dimension of foreign *and* domestic policy, with individuals distributed along the continuum of hawk/conservative to dove/liberal. Decades ago Westerfield (1955) found domestic policy and foreign policy to constitute quite distinct voting dimensions in Congress; a representative's position on one predicted only weakly to position on the other. Russett and Hanson (1975) later reported a substantial degree of merging of the two dimensions in an elite sample, indeed finding that domestic political ideology was a much better predictor of foreign policy attitudes than were various measures of economic interest. They also summarized various other studies, largely of congressional behavior, that provided the same conclusion during the Vietnam war era. Kriesberg and Klein (1980) found much the same, and Holsti and Rosenau's latest work (1988) suggests this phenomenon may have been operating in the mid-1980s.

But to say that one can have some success in predicting hawk-dove attitudes from domestic conservative-liberal ones is not to say that these two dimensions merge closely for most people. They do not. Analysts should not imagine that people's attitudes are confused or inconsistent simply because they do not fit the most common characterizations of academic discourse; many attitude structures are complex and multidimensional. With the rise of social issues (for example, prayer, abortion) and environmental ones to supplement traditional issues of civil rights and income distribution, a mere two or three dimensions cannot cover the full range of domestic and foreign policy concerns. Even the hawk-dove dimension alone is a severe oversimplification. In all their studies Holsti and Rosenau (1984, 1986, 1988; Holsti 1986) documented a fragmentation in foreign policy consensus among American elites, in the sense that a single dimension cannot adequately characterize most people's attitudes. The pattern of fragmentation appears most clearly in their survey conducted in 1976 and weakest in their 1984 survey, but is readily apparent in all of them.

Wittkopf (1987) modifies their findings in substantive detail while essentially supporting the fragmentation thesis. He finds (substantially confirmed by Holsti and Rosenau, 1988) two major dimensions of American foreign policy attitudes: one which divides the opponents and proponents of "cooperative internationalism" according to individuals' readiness to support a broad range of cooperation with other countries and international organizations on trade and development, environment, and arms control issues; and one called "militant internationalism," which is basically a matter of readiness to use military force in pursuit of perceived U.S. global interests. With these two dimensions he can split people into four groups, labeled "hardliners" (favor force but not international cooperation), "internationalists" (favor using force, but in the context of alliances and other international cooperation), "accommodationists" (favor cooperation, oppose use of force), and "isolationists" (prefer to avoid all kinds of international entanglements). Table 4.1 shows this division schematically.

Wittkopf analyzes a variety of national samples of mass attitudes, and samples of elite or "leadership" groups, and finds basically the same two dimensions, and consequently the same structure of attitudes, in all of them. Holsti and Rosenau subsequently confirm this characterization for their 1984 elite study, and other authors find much the same—not only for mass opinion in the United States (Modigliani, 1972; Wittkopf and Maggiotto, 1983; Wittkopf, 1986; Hurwitz and Peffley, 1987; Hinckley, 1988b), but also in Western Europe (Ziegler, 1987).[5] Table 4.2 shows how the various populations seem to have been distributed among the four groups, or quadrants.

The precise percentages have to be taken with a grain of salt, since the samples and questions are only approximately comparable over time. Hinckley's analysis is from a survey con-

Table 4.1. Cooperative internationalism and militant internationalism as dimensions of attitudes on foreign policy.

	Cooperative internationalism	
	Con	Pro
Militant internationalism		
Pro	Hardliners	Internationalists
Con	Isolationists	Accommodationists

Source: Wittkopf, 1987; Holsti and Rosenau, 1988.

5. Dimensions of aggressiveness and involvement appear even in very early attitudes on the Vietnam war; see Russett and Shye, 1990. Wittkopf's results actually suggest the existence of a third dimension, as do those of Hurwitz and Peffley, and Hinckley. Hurwitz and Peffley's sample is drawn only from Lexington, Kentucky, so I have not used it in the subsequent table of national samples. Hinckley divides opponents of cooperative internationalism into isolationists and unilateralists, making six cells for the equivalent table. For my purposes I have recombined them. Whether two or three dimensions are needed to capture the structure of foreign policy attitudes, or precisely how one characterizes their components, is not important for this discussion. The point below about the instability of coalitions when issues are multidimensional would be even stronger for three dimensions than for two.

Table 4.2. The structure of elite and mass attitudes on foreign policy, 1974–1986.

| | Cooperative internationalism | | | | | |
| | Elite samples | | | Mass samples | | |
	Con	Pro	Total	Con	Pro	Total
					1986	
Militant internationalism						
Pro				31	26	57
Con				24	19	43
Total				55	45	100
		1984			1982	
Militant internationalism						
Pro	17	25	42	24	28	52
Con	7	51	58	22	26	48
Total	24	76	100	46	54	100
		1978			1978	
Militant internationalism						
Pro	13	36	49	22	29	51
Con	6	45	51	22	27	49
Total	19	81	100	44	56	100
		1974			1974	
Militant internationalism						
Pro	6	47	53	27	26	53
Con	2	46	48	24	23	47
Total	8	93	100	51	49	100

Sources: for 1986, Hinckley, 1988a; for 1984 elites, Holsti and Rosenau, 1984; all others, Wittkopf, 1987, and personal communication from Wittkopf regarding 1978 mass data.

ducted for the National Strategy Information Center—a relatively conservative group—and the question wording and format may give the appearance of a somewhat more interventionist and noninternationalist mass public than the other studies' procedures would have of the same sample. Moreover, the elite sample is not, and cannot be, considered representative of the weight of different groups or views in the foreign policy process. For instance, the leadership (elite) samples include large numbers of clergy and educators who fall overwhelmingly into the accommodationist quadrant; the most hardline group in the sample is made up of many in the military, business, and law. One may presume that the latter group was more influential in policy-making, especially in 1984. The elite samples are roughly comparable over time, however, making generalizations about trends and change for them, and for the mass public, valuable.

Two things are readily apparent here. First, whereas the essential structure is the same in all samples, the dispersion among the four quadrants is more uniform for the mass public than for the elites. The elites tend to be less interventionist and, especially, more internationalist than the mass public—though, as just noted, this difference is not necessarily represented in relative influence on policy. Second, the pattern of dispersion over time is very stable. In fact, it is remarkably stable among the *general public*: excluding the Hinckley sample, the difference from year to year in any quadrant is rarely more than 3 percent, less than would be expected from sampling errors alone. Here is still further evidence for the stability of public opinion over time.

If opinions at the mass and elite level are structured but multidimensional, the implications for national security policy are profound and in some ways disturbing. Much of the blame for instability in democracies' policy is typically laid at the feet of volatile public moods and opinion changes. We have considered that perspective throughout this chapter, and have repeatedly found it to be a serious misrepresentation of the facts: public opinion on major issues of security policy has not been terribly unstable, either for individuals or for aggregate levels of opinion.

Yet the inability to form a stable majority *in support of policy* need not be rooted in instability of *opinion*. According to the theoretical literature on making public choices (see especially Miller, 1977; Riker, 1984), stable majorities are likely to exist only when preferences are distributed over a single dimension.[6] In foreign policy, for instance, whereas one can assemble a majority behind a particular action (such as uniting all military interventionists behind a limited war), the ability to keep that majority together for a set of actions that crisscross these dimensions

6. Technically the situation is most stable if the preference distribution is single-peaked, but can be stable even in a double-peaked distribution if one peak is substantially larger than the other and remains so over time.

is extremely problematic (for example, supporting the United Nations in a peace-keeping operation or negotiating the terms of a cease-fire with the Soviet Union requires a different coalition, one including the accommodating internationalists). Winning coalitions shift their membership frequently. Neither among the general public nor among the elite is there a single consistent base of support for the whole range of policies which define the country's role in world affairs. Neither mass nor elite is especially culpable for this situation. (There may be a near-majority of accommodationists in these elite samples, but as indicated that does not mean the accommodationists have influence in proportion to their numbers in the samples.)

If everyone were born either a little liberal or a little conservative, whichever group—liberal or conservative—was in the majority would be able to maintain a steady thrust of public policy indefinitely. If most people were concentrated near the middle of the scale, then middle-of-the-road policies would be stable. Only if people switched their ideological preferences, or one side's birth rate were higher than the other's, would that direction of policy change. But if preferences are distributed over more than one dimension there can be *no stable majority coalition even if individual preferences remain fairly stable over time*. Rather, there will be shifting (technically, cyclical) majorities with different winning coalitions; any temporarily "winning" coalition can readily be replaced by another when a different issue becomes prominent. That would be the case not just in a democracy with a mass franchise, but in any pluralistic political system lacking a dictator regularly able to enforce her or his will.

This puts a new light on the connection between national security policy and public opinion. One may well look at the past twenty-five years of American security *policy* and judge it to be volatile in a way that has been unpredictable to Americans, allies, and adversaries alike. That judgment might begin with the breakdown of cold war internationalism during the Vietnam war, the shifts in the first half of the Carter administration and then followed by a more hardline policy in the second half, followed by the further hardline lurch and ultimately return to moderation of the Reagan years. These flip-flops could well be accounted for more by shifts stemming from the multidimensionality of policy preferences than by changing attitudes among the voters. Moreover, if, as we all imagine, the elite has more influence over policy than does the mass, then multidimensionality of preferences among the elites would be more responsible for policy shifts than would the preference structure of the general public. More effectively insulating policy formation from popular influence would then be quite irrelevant as a "solution" to the problem of policy instability.

If a finger of accusation for volatile policy is to be pointed, it should first be directed toward the elites. Upper-status people are on the whole more likely to change their opinions than are members of the general public (Gamson and Modigliani, 1966; Hamilton, 1968; Modigliani, 1972). On many grounds it is desirable that elites should be prepared to change their minds in response to new evidence. Nevertheless, that tendency, plus the important fact that the elites themselves are divided in a multidimensional manner, means they are unable to produce a coherent and stable perspective on means and ends in American foreign policy.

According to the shifting-majority explanation, instability in policy can be reduced only when intellectually or psychologically coherent belief systems emerge to array relevant attitudes along a single dimension—if, for example, most "internationalists" support both multilateral cooperation and military intervention, and most "isolationists" oppose both. That may have been so between World Wars I and II, when isolationists were dominant, and during the first cold war decades, when internationalists were in command. But in the complicated contemporary world such a reordering of belief systems does not happen easily, and sometimes traumatic international events promote fragmentation rather than reduce it (Holsti and Rosenau, 1984). Many would say that such a polarization is simplistic in the contemporary world, and undesirable on its own merits. Perhaps the change in the orientation of American foreign policy wrought by World War II was the last big policy shift attributable to a clear shift in elite and mass opinion.[7]

---

7. Mass and elite opinion surely changed sharply during the Vietnam War, but according to Holsti and Rosenau (also Mandelbaum and Schneider, 1979), by becoming multidimensional rather than giving one clear signal.

On reflection, some degree of instability may not even be such a bad thing, especially if people care intensely about foreign policy. In standard theories of democratic politics, shifting coalitions and crosscutting alliances (across different preference dimensions, with for example isolationists and hardliners allied today, but hardliners and internationalists tomorrow) are thought to be desirable. By preventing any major group from always being in control, shifting coalitions avoid the tyranny of a majority and the polarization, against the system, of permanent losing minorities. Substantial stability is desirable, especially in foreign policy, so a shift of coalitions that empowered extremes would be pernicious. But some change of alignments, still more or less around the center, would be consistent with a prominent model of democratic theory. Here again is an instance of the ability of a leader to put together specific policies from within some range of acceptable options which a majority is prepared to tolerate. Selection of the specific option is an exercise of political leadership, and statesmanship.

5

If All the World Were Democratic

In this Moscow spring, this May 1988, we may be allowed
to hope that freedom . . . will blossom forth at last in the
rich soil of your people and culture. We may be allowed to
hope that the marvelous sound of a new openness will
keep rising through, ringing through, leading to a new
world of reconciliation, friendship, and peace.

Ronald Reagan, address in Moscow

We will do the worst thing to you—we will deprive you of
your enemy.

Georgi Arbatov, to Council on Foreign Relations

Two apparent facts about contemporary international patterns
of war and peace stare us in the face. The first is that some
states expect, prepare for, and fight wars against other states.
The second is that some states do *not* expect, prepare for, or
fight wars *at least against each other*. The first is obvious to
everyone. The second is widely ignored, yet it is now true on a
historically unprecedented scale, encompassing wide areas of the
earth. In a real if still partial sense, peace is already among us.
We need only recognize it, and try to learn from it.

An understanding of why some states do not engage in hostility may lead us to an attainable basis for an alternative system
of security, one that does not depend on acceptance of a world
state to enforce peace or on a particular configuration of strategy
and weaponry to provide a peace of sorts through some form of
stable deterrence. Accordingly, this chapter will explore the
causes, limitations, and implications of this political anomaly
of limited peace already among us.

Peace among Democracies

I refer to the peace among the industrialized and democratically
governed states, primarily in the northern hemisphere. These

states—members of the Organization for Economic Cooperation and Development (OECD: Western Europe, North America, Japan, Australia, and New Zealand), plus a few scattered less-industrialized democratic states—constitute a vast zone of peace, with more than three quarters of a billion people. Not only has there been no war among them for 45 years (see Table 5.1), there has been little expectation of or preparation for war among them either. By war I mean large-scale organized international violence with, by a conventional social science definition, at least 1,000 battle deaths. In fact, even much smaller-scale violence between these countries has been virtually absent. The nearest exception is Greece and Turkey, with their brief and limited violent clashes over Cyprus; they are, however, among the poorest countries of this group, and only sporadically democratic.

In the years before 1945 many of these states fought often and bitterly—but always when at least one of the states in any warring pair was ruled by an authoritarian or totalitarian regime. Despite that past, war among them is now virtually unthinkable. What had been seemingly the most permanent enmities—for instance, between France and Germany—have for the past two or three decades appeared well buried. Individual citizens may not love each other across national boundaries, but neither do they expect the other's state to attack, or wish to mount an attack on it. Expectations of peace are thus equally important; these peoples make few preparations for violence between them; peace for them means more than just the prevention of war through threat and deterrence. This condition has been characterized as

Table 5.1. Distribution of international wars, 1945–1989.

Fought by	Fought in		
	OECD countries	Communist countries	LDCs
OECD countries	0	1	7
Communist countries	0	3	3
LDCs	0	1	19

Source: Small and Singer, 1982, updated to 1989. Includes all interstate and colonial wars (not civil wars) with more than 1000 battle deaths.

a "security community," or as "stable peace" (Deutsch et al., 1957; Boulding, 1979). In duration and expectation it differs from the simple absence of war that may prevail between some other states, including nondemocratic ones in the third world. By the standards of world history this is an extraordinary achievement.

It is not easy to explain just why this peace has occurred. Partly it is due to the network of *international law and institutions* deliberately put into place in order to make a repetition of the previous world wars both unthinkable and impossible. But that network is strongest in Western Europe, often excluding the countries in North America and the Far East; even in the strongest instance the institutions typically lack full powers to police and coerce would-be breakers of the peace; and, as we shall see below, even powerful institutions cannot guarantee peace if the underlying preconditions of peace are lacking.

In part it is due to favorable *economic conditions* associated with advanced capitalism. Fairly steady economic growth, a high absolute level of prosperity, relative equality of incomes within and across the industrial states, and a dense network of trade and investment across national borders all make the resort to violence dubious on cost-benefit grounds; a potential aggressor who already is wealthy risks much from the large-scale destructiveness of modern war, for only moderate gain (Mueller, 1989). But the condition of peace among these rich states has not been endangered by such periods of postwar recession and stagnation as have occurred, and in other parts of the world, especially Latin America, there are democratic states that are not wealthy but are still at peace with one another.

Partly, too, peace is the result of a perceived *"external" threat* faced by the industrialized democracies; they maintain peace among themselves in order not to invite intervention by the communist powers. Where peace among them is threatened, it may be enforced by the dominant "hegemonic" power of the United States (Weede, 1984). But the external threat also has waxed and waned without affecting the peace among these states; indeed, their peace became even more stable during the very time, over the past two decades, when the cold war abated and Europeans, especially, ceased to have much fear of Soviet attack. All these explanations, therefore, are at best only partial ones, and we are driven back to observing that the period of peace among the highly industrialized states essentially coincides with the period when they all have been under democratic rule.[1]

Conceptually and empirically the competing explanations overlap somewhat and reinforce one another, especially for the post–World War II era. International law has served to legitimate widely many of the domestic legal principles of human rights associated with liberal democracy; all advanced capitalist industrial states have been, since World War II, democratic (though not all democratic states are economically advanced); most of them have also been part of the American "hegemonic" alliance system (which has also included nondemocratic and economically less-developed countries). While this overlap prevents a definitive test, all the alternative hypotheses find their predictions falsified by at least one warring pair: the British-Argentine war in 1982, between two capitalist (Argentina only moderately advanced) states allied with the United States. World Wars I and II of course included many industrial capitalist countries as warring pairs. Analysts as different as Joseph Schumpeter and Karl Kautsky predicted peace among advanced capitalist states; Lenin did not. Nor is it simply part of a general statement that politically or culturally similar countries do not fight one another (Russett, 1968, ch. 12; Wilkinson, 1980, ch. 9). An empirical correlation between cultural similarity and relative absence of war exists, but it is a weak one. There are several examples of wars or threats of war within Eastern Europe and Latin America in recent decades; by contrast, a reduction in regional enmities is associated with parallel democratization (for example, Argentina and Brazil).

Another reason to doubt explanations relying chiefly on international institutions, economic conditions, or external threat is that the experience of peace among democratic countries goes back (among fewer countries, to be sure) at least to the end of the Napoleonic wars in 1815. Previous records are less precise,

1. These attempted explanations are considered at greater length in Russett and Starr, 1989, ch. 14. For the European states, Duroselle, 1988, credits democracy and also the demise of colonialism and therefore the end of colonial rivalries. Small and Singer, 1976, p. 67, noted that in their data—ending in 1965—relatively few democracies were contiguous and therefore had much opportunity to fight. Many more contiguous democracies have emerged since then—but no wars.

but also less relevant, since democracy as we know it in this era was at best a rarity before then. In ancient Greece, Athens and Sparta typically allied with democracies and oligarchies respectively. They often intervened to change the domestic constitution of allies to their preferred mode; similarly, a change in domestic constitution among the smaller city-states often produced switches in alliances. Athens did, however, occasionally attack democratic cities, as in Sicily (Fliess, 1966, p. 131).[2]

With only very marginal exceptions, democratic states have not fought one another in the modern era. This is one of the strongest nontrivial or nontautological generalizations that can be made about international relations. The nearest exception is Lebanon's peripheral involvement in Israel's war of independence in 1948. (Israel had not yet held an election, so Small and Singer, 1976, do not count it as a democracy at that time.) Other exceptions are truly marginal: war in 1849 between two states both briefly democratic (France and the Papal States) and Finland against the Allies in World War II (nominally only; Finland's real quarrel was with the USSR). In the war of 1812 with the United States, Britain's franchise was sharply restricted, as was the Boer Republic's in its attempt to preserve its independence against Britain in 1898.

By a democratic state I mean one with the conditions of public contestation and participation, essentially as identified by Robert Dahl (1971), with a voting franchise for a substantial fraction of male citizens (in the nineteenth and early twentieth centuries; wider thereafter), contested elections, and an executive either popularly elected or responsible to an elected legislature. While scholars who have found this pattern differ slightly in their definitions, agreement on the condition of virtual absence of war among democracies ("liberal," "libertarian," or "polyarchic" states) is now overwhelming (Wallensteen, 1973; Small and Singer, 1976; Rummel, 1983, 1985; Chan, 1984; Weede, 1984; Doyle, 1986; Maoz and Abdolali, 1989). This simple fact cries

---

2. In classical and medieval times the state, even in a democracy, was seen as actively shaping society rather than some as impartial arbiter. Hence such states, in addition to sharply restricting the franchise, lacked the modern concept of citizens' natural rights. Thus their behavior provides but an imperfect test of the theory here. See Mansfield, 1983.

out for explanation: What is there about democratic governments that so inhibits their people from fighting one another?

In exploring that question we should be clear about what is
not implied. The condition of peace *between* democratic states
does not mean that democratic states are ipso facto peaceful
with *all* countries. As noted in Chapter 2, they are not. In their
relations with nondemocratic states—whether great powers,
weak states, or non-Western peoples essentially outside the state
system and hence "available" as targets for imperial expansion—
they have often fought, more or less as frequently as nondemocratic states have fought or prepared to fight.

Internal Peace and International Peace

There are powerful norms against the use of lethal force both
within democratic states and between them. Within them is of
course the basic norm of liberal democratic theory—that disputes can be resolved without force through democratic political
processes which in some balance are to ensure both majority
rule and minority rights. A norm of equality operates both as
voting equality and certain egalitarian rights to human dignity.
Democratic government rests on the consent of the governed,
but justice demands that consent not be abused. Resort to organized lethal violence, or the threat of it, is considered illegitimate, and unnecessary to secure one's "legitimate" rights. Dissent within broad limits by a loyal opposition is expected and
even needed for enlightened policymaking, and the opposition's
basic loyalty to the system is to be assumed in the absence of
evidence to the contrary.

All participants in the political process are expected to share
these norms. In practice the norms do sometimes break down,
but the normative restraints on violent behavior—by state and
citizens—are fully as important as the state's monopoly on the
legitimate use of force in keeping incidents of the organized use
of force rare. Democracy is a set of institutions and norms for
peaceful resolution of conflict. The norms are probably more
important than any particular institutional characteristic (two-
party/multiparty, republican/parliamentary) or formal constitutional provision. Institutions may precede the development of
norms. If they do, the basis for restraint is likely to be less secure.

Democracy did not suddenly emerge full-blown in the West, nor by any linear progression. Only over time did it come to mean the extension of a universal voting franchise, formal protection for the rights of ethnic, racial, and religious minorities, and the rights of groups to organize for economic and social action. The rights to organize came to imply the right to carry on conflict—but nonviolently, as by strikes, under the principle that each side in the conflict had to recognize the right of the other to struggle, so long as that struggle was constrained by law, mutual self-interest, and mutual respect. The implicit or explicit contract in the extension of such rights was that the beneficiaries of those rights would in turn extend them to their adversaries.

To observe this is not to accept democratic theory uncritically, or to deny that it is part of a belief structure that, in Gramsci's view of cultural hegemony, may serve to legitimate dominant-class interests and provide subordinate classes with a spurious sense of their own political efficacy.[3] As such, it may exaggerate belief in the "reasonableness" of both the demands of one's own state in international politics and those of other democratic states. But it is precisely beliefs and perceptions that are primarily at issue here; insofar as the other state's demands are considered ipso facto reasonable according to a view of one's own system that extends to theirs, popular sentiment for war or resistance to compromise is undermined.

Politics within a democracy is seen as a largely nonzero-sum enterprise: by cooperating, all can gain something even if all do not gain equally, and the winners today are restrained from crushing the losers; indeed, the winners may, with shifting coalitions, wish tomorrow to ally with today's losers. If the conflicts degenerate to physical violence, either by those in control of the state or by insurgents, all can lose. In international politics—the anarchy of a self-help system with no superordinate governing authority—these norms are not the same. "Realists" remind us of the powerful norms of legitimate self-defense and the acceptability of military deterrence, norms much more extensive inter-

---

3. If one or both governments is not broadly representative despite the cultural belief that it is, the possibility of irreconcilable conflicts of interest between them is increased.

nationally than within democratic states. Politics between nations takes on a more zero-sum hue. True, we know we all can lose in nuclear war or in a collapse of international commerce, but we worry much more about comparative gains and losses. The essence of "realist" politics is that even when two states both become more wealthy, if one gains much more wealth than the other it also gains more power, more potential to coerce the other; thus the one which is lagging economically only in relative terms may be an absolute loser in the power contest.

The principles of anarchy and self-help in a zero-sum world are seen most acutely in "structural realist" theories of international relations. Specifically, a bipolar system of two great states or alliances, each much more powerful than any others in the international system, is seen as inherently antagonistic. The nature of the great powers' internal systems of government is irrelevant; whatever they may work out with or impose on some of their smaller allies, their overall behavior with other great powers is basically determined by the structure of the international system and their position in that structure. Athens and Sparta, or the United States and the Soviet Union, are doomed to compete and to resist any substantial accretion to the other's power. To fail to compete is to risk the death of sovereignty, or death itself. Through prudence and self-interest they may avoid a full-scale war that might destroy or cripple both of them (the metaphor of two scorpions in a bottle), but the threat of war is never absent, and can never be absent. "Peace," such as it is, can come only from deterrence, eternal vigilance, and probably violent competition between their "proxies" elsewhere in the world. By this structural realist understanding, the kind of stable peace that exists between the democratic countries can never exist on a global scale (Waltz, 1979).

Efforts to establish norms against the use of lethal violence internationally have been effective only to a limited degree. The Kellogg-Briand Pact of 1928 to outlaw war was a failure from the outset, as have been efforts to outlaw "aggressive" war. Despite its expression of norms and some procedures for the pacific settlement of disputes, the United Nations Charter fully acknowledges "the inherent right of individual or collective self-defense if an armed attack occurs" (Article 51). It could hardly do otherwise in the absence of superordinate authority. The norm of national self-defense—including collective self-defense on behalf of allies, and defense of broadly conceived "vital" interests even when national survival is not at stake—remains fully legitimate to all but tiny pacifist minorities. While there is some cross-cultural variation in the readiness of different peoples to use lethal force in different modes of self-defense, these differences are not strongly linked to form of government. Citizens of small democracies who perceive themselves as beleaguered (such as Israel), or citizens of large powerful democracies with imperial histories or a sense of global responsibilities for the welfare of others (such as Britain or the United States) are apt to interpret national or collective interest quite broadly. Especially across international cultural barriers, perversions of the "right" of self-defense come easily.

Yet democratic peoples exercise that right within a sense that somehow they and other peoples *ought* to be able to satisfy common interests and work out compromise solutions to their problems, without recourse to violence or threat of it. After all, that is the norm for behavior to which they aspire within democratic systems. Since other people living in democratic states are presumed to share those norms of live and let live, they can be presumed to moderate their behavior in international affairs as well. That is, they can be respected as self-governing peoples, and expected to offer the same respect to other democratic countries in turn. The habits and predispositions they show in their behavior in internal politics can be presumed to apply when they deal with like-minded outsiders. If one claims the principle of self-determination for oneself, normatively one must accord it to others perceived as self-governing. Norms do matter. Within a transnational democratic culture, as within a democratic nation, others are seen as possessing rights and exercising those rights in a spirit of enlightened self-interest. Acknowledgment of those rights both prevents us from wishing to dominate them and allows us to mitigate our fears that they will try to dominate us.

Realism has no explanation for the fact that certain kinds of states—namely, democratic ones—do not fight or prepare to fight one another. One must look instead to the liberal idealist vision of Immanuel Kant's *Perpetual Peace*, embodied also in Woodrow

Wilson's vision of a peaceful world of democratic states. This same vision inspired American determination to root out fascism and establish the basis for democratic governments in West Germany and Japan after World War II (and partly also explains and was used to justify interventions in Vietnam, Grenada, Nicaragua, and so on).

Democratic states, with their wide variety of active interest groups in shifting coalitions, also present the opportunity for the formation of transnational coalitions in alliance with groups in other democracies. This may seem a form of "meddling"; it also provides another channel for resolution of international conflict. International anarchy is not supplanted by institutions of common government, but conflicts of interest within the anarchy can be moderated fairly peacefully on the principle of self-determination within an international society.

How much importance should we attribute to perceptions among the public in general, and how much to those of the elites including, in particular, the leaders of the state? Decisions for war, and indeed most major decisions in national security matters, are taken by the leaders and debated largely among the elites. They have some ability to mold mass opinion. Nevertheless, the elites in a democracy know that the expenditure of blood and treasure in any extended or costly international conflict will not be popular, and can be sustained only with the support of the general public. Whereas there may be leads and lags either way, we saw in Chapter 4 that long-term serious differences between public opinion and official foreign policy are rare. Hence the elites will be somewhat constrained by popular views of the reasonableness of engaging in violent conflict with a particular foreign country.

In some ways the principle of self-determination may actually work better in the absence of a common government. If there were a set of central institutions for common government, different groups and peoples would by necessity compete to control them, with the risk that control (majority rule) would be abused at the expense of minority rights. A common government would have the legal right and powers to tax, to coerce, to reallocate wealth and benefits. For the institutions to work peaceably the norms must be strong and widely shared. In the absence of broad agreement on politics and culture, it is best that the institutions, and the possibility for their abuse, also be absent. Hence some peoples can live with one another peaceably under separate governments but not under a common one. (Contrast, for example, relations between Protestant Britain and Catholic Ireland with those between Protestants and Catholics within Northern Ireland, or the American North and South where the issues had to be settled with a terrible civil war.) The formal institutions of democratic government might be in place under a common state, but the degree of sharing in the norms of self-restraint, and confidence that others share those norms, would be inadequate to insure peace. Hence also comes the common fear of a world leviathan containing very diverse peoples, *even* under some form of direct election and representation. The norms might well be insufficient to restrain action, especially given the extreme economic inequalities of the contemporary global community.

Relations with Nondemocratic States

When we look within the construct of democratic ideology, it is apparent that the restraints on behavior that operate between separately governed democratic peoples do not apply to their relations with nondemocratic states. If other self-governing (democratic) peoples can be presumed to be worthy of being treated in a spirit of compromise and as in turn acting in that spirit, the same presumption does not apply to authoritarian states. According to democratic norms, authoritarian states do not rest on the proper consent of the governed, and thus they cannot properly represent the will of their peoples—if they did, they would not need to rule through undemocratic, authoritarian institutions. Rulers who control their own people by such means, who do not behave in a just way that respects their own people's right to self-determination, cannot be expected to behave better toward peoples outside their states. "Because nonliberal governments are in a state of aggression with their own people, their foreign relations become for liberal governments deeply suspect. In short, fellow liberals benefit from a presumption of amity; nonliberals suffer from a presumption of enmity" (Doyle, 1986, p. 1161). Authoritarian governments are expected to aggress against others if given the power and the opportunity. By this reasoning, democracies must be eternally vigilant against them, and may even sometimes feel the need to engage in preemptive or preventive (defensively motivated) war against them.

Whereas wars against other democratic states are neither expected nor considered legitimate, wars against authoritarian states may often be expected and "legitimated" by the principles outlined above. Thus an international system composed of both democratic and authoritarian states will include both zones of peace (actual and expected, among the democracies) and zones of war or at best deterrence between democratic states and authoritarian ones and, of course, between authoritarian states. Two states may avoid war even if one of them is not a democracy, but chiefly because of the power of one or both states to deter the other from the use of lethal force: the one-sided deterrence of dominance, or mutual deterrence between those more or less equally powerful. If the democratic state is strong, its "forbearance" may permit war to be avoided.

Of course, democracies have not fought wars only out of motivations of self-defense, however broadly one may define self-defense to include "extended deterrence" for the defense of allies and other interests or to include anticipation of others' aggression. Many of them have also fought imperialist wars to acquire or hold colonies (like the French in Vietnam) or, since World War II, to retain control of states formally independent but within their spheres of influence (like the Americans in Vietnam). In these cases they have fought against people who on one ground or another could be identified as not self-governing.[4]

In the nineteenth-century days of colonial expansion, the colonized peoples were in most instances outside the European state system. They were in most instances not people with white skins. And they were in virtually every instance people whose institutions of government did not conform to the Western democratic institutional forms of their democratic colonizers. Europeans' ethnocentric views of those peoples carried the *assumption* that they did not have instititions of self-government, that their governments or tribal leaders were not just or consensual.

---

4. There also have been cases of covert intervention (rather than overt attack) against some radical but elected Third World governments (Guatemala, Chile) justified by a cold war ideology and public belief that the government in question was allying itself with the major nondemocratic adversary.

They were not merely available as candidates for imperial aggrandizement, they could also be considered candidates for betterment and even "liberation"—the white man's burden, or *mission civilatrice*. Post-Darwinian ideology even regarded them as at a lower stage of physical evolution and intellectual capacity than whites (and especially white males: Arendt, 1952; Vincent, 1984; C. Russett, 1989). They could be brought the benefits not only of modern material civilization, but of Western principles of self-government and, after proper tutelage, of the institutions of self-government. If they did not have such institutions already, then by definition they were already being exploited and repressed. Their governments or tribal leaders could not, in this ethnocentric view, be presumed to be just or consensual, and thus one need have few compunctions about conquering them. They were legitimate candidates for "liberal" imperialism.

Later, Western forms of self-government did begin to take root at least on a local basis in the colonies; the extremes of pseudo-Darwinian racism lost their legitimacy. As these things happened, the legitimacy of the colonial powers in controlling those peoples was eroded. Indeed, indigenous leaders vigorously turned back onto their colonial rulers their very own principles (for example, independence leaders in the Philippines; or Gandhi and the Congress Party in India, who were especially effective normatively against a British Labour government deeply committed to providing equality at home). Decolonization came about not only because the colonial governments had lost the power to retain their colonies but also because in many cases they lost confidence in their normative right to rule. The evolution of the colonies themselves—and of the understandings about colonial peoples that were held in the imperial states—eroded the legitimacy of the colonial rulers in their own eyes. The imperial peoples' liberal principles were turned back on them. In a further round, those principles are now being turned against Third World authoritarian rulers.[5]

Another important caution must take account of scapegoating, as discussed in Chapter 2. It is an old trick to blame outsiders—

5. Aid to the Nicaraguan contras was never really popular in the United States, not just because of realpolitik fears of "another Vietnam," but because of a general perception that the contras were no more legitimate or representative of their people than were the Sandinistas.

either socially marginal groups within a country or external
adversaries—when things go wrong. It is often popular to attribute troubles to foreigners, or to try to turn people's frustrations
against external enemies, whether or not those outside can plausibly be blamed for the troubles. This kind of behavior has long
been attributed to dictatorships, with examples including Nazi
persecution of Germany's Jews and the Argentine junta's decision, in 1982, to stoke popular nationalism over the Falkland/
Malvinas islands at a time of economic stagnation and political
unrest. Ironically, however, certain forms of scapegoating behavior—notably the rally 'round the flag effect—may be equally
prevalent in democracies. The tendency to scapegoat may be
strengthened by the very virtue of democracy in giving to the
mass public a degree of control over their fate: mass opinion is
typically less informed, and in some real sense more ethnocentric and less cosmopolitan, than elite opinion. That ethnocentrism may be magnified when confronted by conflicts with other
peoples who are not governed "like us."

A Shift Toward Democracy

The end of World War II brought in its wake the demise of
colonial empires; it brought a degree of self-determination to the
formerly colonized peoples. Unfortunately, that self-determination was often highly restricted, limited in part by ties of economic and military "neocolonialism." Self-determination also
was often limited to the elites of the new states, as the governments installed were frequently authoritarian and repressive,
anything but democratic. Yet there has been, over the period of
about the last decade and a half, some evolution toward greater
frequency of democracy in large parts of what is called the Third
World. In late 1973 only two Spanish- or Portugese-speaking
states in South America were governed by democratic regimes
(Colombia and Venezuela); now only two are ruled by military
dictatorships (Chile and Paraguay, both now in transition).
"Democracy" remains fragile and imperfect in many of them,[6]
but the relative shift away from authoritarian rule is palpable.

6. O'Donnell, 1988, for example, characterizes Brazil as in danger of becoming a

Table 5.2. World percentage distribution of states by degree of political freedom, 1973, 1976, 1988.

	1973	1976	1988
Free	32	30	35
Partly free	24	32	32
Not free	44	39	33
Number of states	165	165	165

Source: Gastil, 1989. Gastil has rated the same states over time, not adding new ones except for the European Community as a whole (I count only the member states) and Transkei (I exclude as not independent), and splitting Cyprus into Greek and Turkish halves after 1982 (I still count as one unit, since he codes them the same).

This shift shows up statistically on a worldwide basis. A long-time observer of political rights and civil liberties has carried out, over this period, a project of rating countries according to their degree of "political freedom" (Gastil, 1989, and previous editions). His rating is not meant to reflect a broad definition of human rights that includes, for example, the "second generation" economic rights to employment or the satisfaction of basic physical needs. Rather, it addresses "first generation" rights: electoral practices, the accountability of the executive and the legislature, judicial procedures, and freedom of expression and association—in short, dimensions of the traditional political definition of democracy. For some of his purposes he uses two scales of seven points each; for others he collapses these complex judgments into three categories of states: free, partly free, and not free. The distribution of states in these three categories has varied over time, as shown in Table 5.2.

By Gastil's evaluation, there has been a substantial decline in the number of strongly authoritarian (not free) states and a similarly substantial increase in the number of partly free states. There has also been a clear though smaller increase in the number of free states, especially if 1973 is used as the base year.[7]

"democradura," that is, "a civilian government controlled by military and authoritarian elements."

7. In the most recent edition the author abandons his earlier three-part rating and relies solely on the 14-point scale. For our purposes, however, it is appropriate to maintain his previous equation of scores 2–5 with "free," 6–11 with "partly free," and 12–14 with "not free." Overall, one can argue with elements of his ranking

These trends can be seen in many parts of the world: the demise of dictatorships in Greece, Portugal, and Spain; his recent characterization of Hungary, Poland, and even the Soviet Union with scores in the "partly free" range; improvements in China (as of 1988, and still basically "not free"); and shifts in several large, important countries elsewhere—Argentina, Brazil, India (since 1976 and its "emergency rule"), Pakistan, the Philippines, South Korea, Thailand, and Uganda.

The degree of democratization should not be exaggerated, and the most substantial increase is only in the "partly free" category. The first shifts—to popular access to alternative sources of information and relative freedom of expression—are the easiest, and costly for governments to suppress. Pressure to cross further thresholds of democratization—the development of alternative political organizations, and of free, fair elections—represents a greater threat to governmental power; these steps may seem to follow inexorably and yet may meet with stiffer resistance from the state (Dahl, 1988). Whatever the ultimate outcome, recent developments may indicate more than just a cyclical alternation of democracy and dictatorship in an extension of the fluctuations of the 1930s and early 1970s. Rather, they may be an extension of a very long-term trend of global norms produced by the succession, since the seventeenth century, of powerful nations with increasingly democratic internal political systems (the Dutch Republic, Britain, and the United States; see Modelski, 1988). Some influences operating in the Philippines case of 1986 may suggest similar conditions which can reinforce movements toward democracy elsewhere:

1. The "demonstration" or "contagion" effect of the restoration of democracy in a number of states, especially in Latin

---

system, but for our purposes most of these arguments are not relevant. It has been applied quite consistently over the years, except that the author suggests he probably should not have coded several Latin American states (Colombia, El Salvador, and Guatemala) as "free" in 1973. If so, however, that inconsistency *understates* the shift toward democracy indicated by the above table. His judgments also agree well with independent judgments by Michael Coppedge and Wolfgang Reinecke, "A Scale of Polyarchy," in Gastil, 1988, and by Dahl, 1971, Appendix B, note 8 and authors cited in footnote 6. Increasing adoption of democratic institutions does not, however, mean the United States version of federalism, separation of powers, etc. See Beyme, 1987.

America, sharing important cultural characteristics with the Philippines.

2. Belated but still effective political intervention by the United States against continuation of the Marcos regime.

3. The role of national and international television—cleverly exploited by the revolutionaries, who made seizure of the television station a prime objective—which brought the full glare of publicity onto any violent government supression of the demonstrators. Globally observed bloodshed would have further undermined Marcos's already fading legitimacy; yet his failure to order violent suppression of the demonstrators permitted their success.

4. The role of international organizations in protecting, deliberately or otherwise, key centers of opposition to the regime. Cardinal Sin's position was especially critical (Hanson, 1987.)

5. The role of expatriates (especially Filipinos in Hawaii and the mainland United States) in providing experience and financial support to the opposition.

Obviously these influences do not apply equally to all cases, but one can observe them in lesser degree in places as different as East Germany and South Korea. All these illustrate instruments by which developing international norms about political rights can be made effective.

Arguably the shift to democracy is substantially a result of the manifest economic as well as political failures of dictatorships: authoritarian regimes instituted in the name of economic growth and national development which were unable to deliver on their promises. Perhaps after a spurt of economic growth, they all too often brought stagnation, greater economic inequality, and a loss of true national autonomy, in addition to the suppression of political liberties. It is no wonder that they lost favor with their peoples. Democratic governments also may ultimately lose favor if they are unable to revive stagnant economies—an especially severe danger in Latin America, though many peoples have so far shown a good deal of tolerance for their governments' predicament. Economic failures, in communist as well as capitalist states, might ultimately increase support for nationalist, fundamentalist, or fascist ideologies rather than for democracy. For now we can perhaps be permitted a degree of hopefulness, and even an assertion that authoritarian rule is out of favor in the global culture, with effects in communist countries and in the Third World.

It can always be a cause for rejoicing when people gain more power over their own fate, with a widening and deepening of the institutions and practices of democratic government. Does this analysis imply something more, that if the shift toward democracy does continue we will move toward an era of international peace? If all states were democratic could we all live in perpetual peace? Does a solution to international violence lie in creating a world in which all countries are governed by democratic practices? In principle, this would both rid the world of the aggressive behavior of some kinds of autocratic regimes and deprive democratically governed peoples of a normatively legitimate target for jingoism.

A serious reservation, however, must concern interpretation of the word "creating." The argument here does *not* imply that the route to ultimate perpetual peace is through wars, or threats of war, to make other countries democratic. World War II may in that sense have been a success with Japan and West Germany, but who would want to repeat the experience against a contemporary great power? External threats all too commonly become means to reinforce, not relax, the repressive power of the state. Wars are corrupting to those who fight them, serving to legitimate violence within as well as between countries (Stein, 1980). The self-righteous temptation to blame the adversary and dehumanize the enemy is too strong to give any encouragement to a crusading "holy war" mentality. The degrading experience of western imperialism, alone, should be enough to discourage efforts to force other peoples to be free. Such efforts are likely to be neither just nor successful.

A second temptation, related to the first, may be to define "democracy" too narrowly and ethnocentrically, equating it too readily with all the particular norms and institutions of the Western parliamentary tradition. True, the norms and institutions of democracy as Westerners know it have provided powerful restraints on absolutism. They can be treated as *an* effective model for others to adopt. But it is better for other countries to adapt those norms and institutions to the conditions of their own histories and cultures than to adopt them as copied from a Western template. If the goal is a world in which all peoples experience a high degree of self-determination and consent of the governed, norms and institutions that flow out of non-Western peoples' histories may succeed where particular Western forms would not. For this line of thinking we should relax the rigorous (and consciously ethnocentric) operational definition of democracy used early in this chapter.

It is inexcusably ethnocentric to imagine that other peoples are inherently incapable of autonomy and self-government, to declare them unsuited for democracy. While it is myopic to overlook or idealize the ways in which many Third World governments, for instance, oppress their own peoples, it is equally ethnocentric to imagine that their ways of ensuring autonomy and self-determination will be exactly like ours, or to require the full panoply of western forms. In terms of the vision here, what is important is to support democratic governments where they exist and to recognize and reinforce a worldwide movement toward greater popular control over governments, rather than to specify the endpoint in detail for each case.

Human Rights and Information

Whatever the faults of Western liberal (bourgeois) democracy, a world of spreading democratic ideology and practice offers some significant possibilities also for spreading peace. Those possibilities can be enhanced by attention to implementing a broad definition of human rights and institutionalizing a freer flow of information.[8] Human rights and information are elements both of greater global democratization and of direct and indirect contributions to international peace. In a world of imperfect democratization, such elements can help reduce those imperfections, and can compensate for some of them in the avoidance of war.

1. Recent American governments have tended, in different ways, to emphasize a commitment to human rights. In the Carter administration this began with an emphasis on political

8. Any discussion of human rights, as of democracy, is inevitably colored by one's historical context, including mine as a privileged member of society in a powerful capitalist country, governed by democratic procedures as understood in the Western liberal tradition. My perspective on these matters is nevertheless one of moderate historicism: that whereas all are in some sense conventions, they can be substantially grounded across ages and cultures. See Bernstein, 1983, and Haskell, 1987.

rights and civil liberties throughout the world; American standards were applied both to communist countries and to Third World states. Those governments found wanting did not appreciate the criticism. American attention to human rights in the Soviet Union reflected and perhaps hastened the decline of détente; despite some successes in the Third World American pressures often angered allies thought to be strategically important, and the pressures were lessened. During the early years of the Reagan administration, official policy on human rights seemed to be turned most critically toward the Soviet Union and its allies, with abuses by American allies typically overlooked, tolerated, or even abetted. American allies were said to be merely authoritarian states, not totalitarian ones. The frequent ineffectiveness or hypocrisy of American policy on human rights has given the whole concept a bad name to some otherwise sympathetic and liberal-minded people. But the forces strengthening human rights can at least be assisted by low-key persuasion and good example.

Efforts to promote human rights internationally have not been uniformly ineffective or hypocritical. Third world states sometimes do relax the worst of their oppression in response to external pressures, whether those pressures come from governments, international organizations, or private transnational organizations like Amnesty International and Americas Watch. External pressures can contribute to the legitimacy of internal opposition. Some of the rhetoric and liberalizing action of Gorbachev owes a great debt to the power and attractiveness of Western concepts of human rights. Western efforts to reiterate those concepts and their implications—for Eastern Europe as well as for the Soviet Union itself—can hardly be abandoned. An image of the Soviet government as willing to grant a fairly high degree of autonomy to its own citizens but not to its neighbors would hardly fit the image of a state with the "liberal," "live-and-let-live" policy essential to the basis of international peace being discussed in these pages.

Yet political concessions in the form of domestic human rights policies cannot be *demanded* of another great power. The principle of noninterference in the internal governance of other states (in international law, statist and positivist norms), dating from the end of the Thirty Years War, does help to defuse one major source of interstate conflict and cannot lightly be cast aside. Hectoring or badgering the leaders of another great power is likely to poison political relations and exacerbate other conflicts; linkage of human rights concessions to important arms control measures is likely to hobble efforts to reduce real dangers of inadvertent escalation of conflict. The failure to reach human rights goals should not become a reason to forgo arms control agreements or, worse, used as an excuse to prevent arms control agreements.

International discussions on human rights are properly a dialogue, wherein the normatively persuasive elements are not solely those of Western advocates. A broad conception of human rights most certainly requires great emphasis on the kind of political rights stressed in American statements. Movement toward a more democratic world requires continued repetition of that message. It also requires a recognition of the legitimacy of some of the rights stressed by others: economic rights, to employment, housing, and some basic standard of material life (Beitz, 1979; Kim, 1984.) Justice demands political liberty, and it also demands a decent level of economic well-being. Political and social peace within democratic countries has been bought in part by this recognition; severe dismantlement of the welfare state would inflame class and ethnic conflict, and most elected political leaders know it. Internationally, recognition of the multifaceted nature of human rights is essential if the dialogue is to be one of mutual comprehension and persuasion. This is a way in which political rights, economic rights, and international peace are bound inextricably together.

Increasing worldwide adherence to democratic political norms and practices cannot alone bear all the weight of sustaining peace. Greater prosperity and economic justice, especially in the Third World, must also bear a major part. This conviction has often been expressed (for example, Brandt, 1980; Shue, 1980); cynics often dismiss it. But it is unlikely to be merely a coincidence that, as noted earlier, the industrial democracies are rich as well as democratic. The distribution of material rewards within them, while hardly ideal, is nevertheless far more egalitarian than that within many Third World countries, or between

First and Third World peoples. That relatively just distribution does affect the cost-benefit analysis of those who would drastically alter it by violence; both rich and poor know they could lose badly. Some such calculation, including but not limited to the normative demands of justice, must apply to cement peace between nations. The broader human rights dialogue, incorporating political, cultural, and economic rights, constitutes a key element of global democratization where the domestic institutions of democracy are imperfect.

2. Another aspect of a stable international peace—reinforcing but not fully contained in concepts of political democracy and human rights—concerns practices and institutions for international communication and cooperation. This has several elements.

One is *economic*: a freer flow of goods and services between communist and capitalist countries, especially including the Soviet Union. Henry Kissinger's détente policy envisaged such a network of interdependence, giving the Soviet Union a greater material stake in peaceful relations with the capitalist world, and increased Soviet interest in Western products and markets makes the vision all the more plausible. The vision is consistent with traditional liberal prescriptions for trade and international cooperation (Rosecrance, 1986). While it is not a sufficient condition for peace, and possibly not even a necessary one, it certainly can make an important contribution.

Economic exchange is also a medium and an occasion for the exchange of *information*. Facilitation of a freer flow of information is a second major element. Without a free flow of information outward there can be no confidence in the outside world that democratic practices are really being followed within a country, and sharp restrictions on the flow of information into one's own country are incompatible with the full democratic competition of ideas inside it. Cultural exchanges and free travel across state boundaries can help ease misunderstandings of the other's reasoning, goals, and intent. Across the spectrum from academic game theory to concrete social experience, we know that the prospects for cooperation are much enhanced if the relevant actors can communicate their preferences and actions clearly. This too is not a sufficient condition, and it is easy to trivialize or ridicule the idea by imagining that communication alone can solve international problems. But without the dependable exchange of information, meaningful cooperation is virtually impossible in a world of complex problems and complex national governing systems.[9]

It is in this sense that *institutions*—especially what Keohane (1984) calls "information rich" institutions—are valuable as a means to discover and help achieve shared and complementary interests. Global organizations such as UN agencies are important purveyors of relevant information. Regional organizations, especially among culturally similar countries, may be much less important as instruments of coercion or enforcement than as a means of spotlighting major human rights violations and upholding the moral force of higher norms. The European Commission on Human Rights and the European Court of Human Rights have done this effectively, the Inter-American Commission on Human Rights and the Inter-American Court of Human Rights to a lesser degree (Weston et al., 1987). Transnational and populist legal norms serve to counter statist ones, and principles of democratic rights become incorporated, often through treaties, into international law and thereby into other states' domestic law (see MacDougal et al., 1980; Falk, 1981; Boyle, 1985).

The element of information exchange relates directly to progress on *security* issues. Arms control and disarmament agreements require confidence that compliance with the agreements can be verified. Arrangements for ensuring verification must be established on a long-term, reliable basis. Without verification the agreements are continually hostage both to real fears that the agreements are being violated and to pernicious charges by those who are opposed to the agreements whether or not they are being violated. An authoritarian government can more easily, if it wishes, pursue long-term strategies of aggressive expansion than can a pluralistic democracy with many power centers and voices. "Democratic governments can also have their military buildups, of course, but cannot mask them because a public atmosphere of fear or hostility will have to be created to justify the sacrifices; they can threaten other countries, but only after

---

9. A balanced assessment of functionalist benefits in the range of Soviet-American exchanges is Jangotch, 1985. In a very different context, see Russett, 1963. Specifically on the conflict-reducing effects of East-West trade, see Gasiorowski and Polachek, 1982.

their action has been justified in the open." (Luttwak, 1987, p. 235). Liberalization of the Soviet Union allows its external partners and adversaries to feel less apprehensive, and to feel more confident that they will have early warning of any newly aggressive policy.

A dense, informal network of information exchange which extends across a wide range of issues and is beyond the control of any government will help, as will some formal institutions for information-sharing. Just as substantial freedom of information is essential to democratic processes within a country, it is essential to peaceful collaboration between autonomous, self-determining peoples organized as nation-states.

Certain specific kinds of multilateral institutions can be important in controlling crises. One possibility is to create crisis management centers, of the kind already established by the United States and the Soviet Union but extended to include other nuclear powers whose actions might cascade a crisis. Another is to strengthen the information and communications base—now sadly inadequate—of the United Nations, and especially of the Secretary General, so that in some future event like the Cuban missile crisis he could act as an informed and timely mediator. Yet another possibility is to have observation satellites operated by third parties (other countries, or international organizations) to monitor military activities and arms control compliance by a variety of electronic means (Boudreau, 1984; Florini, 1988). As long as nuclear weapons exist, even in a world of substantial political liberalization, reliable means of information exchange will be essential.

The Coming Test?

Democracies, as well as other political systems, do have their dark side of externalizing popular frustrations, and some degree of xenophobia is virtually universal. The United States and the Soviet Union, as multi-ethnic societies, are perhaps especially prone to defining patriotism in terms of loyalty more to the political system than to a set of cultural principles. Democracy and socialism thus become defining principles for identifying friends and foes. A shift away from seeing the other as the enemy will not come easily (Shaw and Wong, 1988), though it may be assisted by change within the Soviet system which blurs the existing differences of political practice.

The winds of democracy are blowing in the world, even if in gusts of variable strength and direction. Recently they have become especially evident in the communist countries, and dramatically so with *glasnost* and *perestroika* in the Soviet Union. The current depth and long-term prospects for this movement are highly uncertain. Here too, the twin dangers of wishful thinking and willful ignorance about these events are unavoidably present. The Soviet Union may not soon become a liberal democracy as people in the West understand that term. The bureaucratic, cultural, and historical constraints are powerful. But democratization as a process is (as of late 1989) surely occurring.

There is greater freedom of expression and dissent within the Soviet Union now, and more competition for political control. There is greater openness across the Soviet Union's international borders, for the transmission of ideas and information into as well as out from the country. Prospects for increased trade and cultural exchange can help solidify this openness. Mikhail Gorbachev is explicitly asking his country to adopt some Western norms, as desirable in themselves and as legitimating economic and political modernization. This is an exhilarating and uncertain process, perhaps subject to some reversal but not easily controllable by any leader or group. "Before behaviorial revolutions come conceptual revolutions," and the ideological structure of class warfare, centralized Soviet power, and inevitable communist triumph is now shattered beyond reconstruction (Legvold, 1988/89, p. 83).

An article of faith of the dominant ideologies in both the United States and the Soviet Union has always been that neither has any fundamental quarrel with the people of the other country. American differences allegedly have been not with the Soviet people, but with the atheistic communist elites that repress the people; alternatively, Soviet differences have been not with the American people but with the greedy capitalist elites who exploit them. Insofar as the Soviet system of government operated under principles so manifestly different from those of Western democracy, the American claim had a prima facie validity.[10]

---

10. Almost 90 percent of Americans believe that the Russian people are not as

And insofar as the Soviet leadership explicitly rejected the legitimacy of Western democracy as representing the interests of its peoples, their claim also seemed valid to their people. Now, as Soviet ideology and practice begin to shift, the distinction between ruling elites and their people loses some of its force. If both sides see each other as in some sense truly reflecting the rule of law and the consent of the governed, the transformation of international relations begins. A high official in the Soviet foreign ministry has said:

> Nor can there be any trust in dictatorial, anti-popular regimes which are all but inevitably spreading methods of violence beyond their national borders as well . . . And why were our partners frightened by Stalinism? There are many reasons, but one is perfectly clear; i.e., it is difficult to have confidence in a society which is mired in all-out suspicion, it is hard to trust a regime that has no faith in its own people (Kozyrev, 1988, p. 3).

Realist theories about the inherently antagonistic structure of international relations have never been tested in a world where all the major states were governed more or less democratically. Thus we never have had a proper test of some realist propositions against liberal idealist ones.[11] Perhaps we are about to see one. Even if liberal idealist theories are correct, it is not clear whether some threshold of democratic norms and practices must be crossed to achieve peace, or whether (Rummel, 1983, 1985) it is merely a matter of greater *degree* of democratization bringing a greater *likelihood* of peace between states. It is also not clear what ancillary conditions must be met, or whether sufficient

---

hostile to the United States as are their leaders, and that the Russians could be our friends if the attitude of their leaders were different. Yankelovich and Harman, 1988, p. 64, citing a December 1983 survey. Evarts, 1989, reports that large majorities in all major West European states but France agreed that "real and positive changes have taken place in the Soviet Union."

11. Neither realist nor liberal idealist theories are fully adequate, but the dominance of realist thinking in contemporary academic as well as government circles has tended to diminish attention to realism's analytical and empirical weaknesses. See Nye, 1988; Vasquez, 1988. Note that the theoretical perspective of this chapter attends neither to the international-system level of analysis nor to the individual nation-state, but rather to the nature of *relations* between two states. For the distinction, see Russett and Starr, 1989, ch. 1. The whole analysis of this book, that domestic politics importantly influence foreign policy, is outside the mainstream of realist thinking.

democratization in the Soviet Union can in fact be reached by anything that can evolve from its domestic history and the cold war. A hint, however, is that among characteristics deemed "absolutely necessary" for cooperative relations in mid-1988, only 29 percent of Americans insisted that the other country be "a democracy," but 53 percent required that it be one where "citizens enjoy basic human rights" (Yankelovich and Smoke, 1988, p. 16).

Perhaps two or more great powers can exist in the same international system where, governed by self-interest and some sense of broader interest but not ruled by any superordinate authority, they can build conditions for the avoidance of war that do not depend primarily on nuclear deterrence and military threat. In such a situation, nuclear weapons might continue to exist, but crises would occur less often and, when they did, would carry less weighty ideological baggage. From the perspective of the cold warriors on both sides of what was called the Iron Curtain, the really subversive nature of *glasnost* may be that it will make the Soviet Union no longer eligible for "the presumption of enmity."

6

Sustaining Sensible Policy

It is true that a democratic regime runs the risk that the people will make mistakes. But the risk exists in all regimes in the real world, and the worst blunders of this century have been made by leaders in non-democratic regimes.

Robert A. Dahl, *Controlling Nuclear Weapons: Democracy versus Guardianship*

Political theorists have long been divided between those who trust the masses and those who fear or despise them. The divergence may also occur within the same head: an ambivalence between an anxiety that mass opinions will be based on ignorance and emotion, at best fickle and at worst dangerously misguided, and a fear that the alternatives to mass control—one form or another of oligarchy—are even more dangerous. Discussions of national security policy exemplify the force of this divergence. Can something as vital to the life and independence of the nation safely be left to popular decision—and if something so central to the lives of individuals is to be alienated from popular control, does "democracy" any longer have much meaning?

Secrecy and Participation

The debate is as old as democratic government itself; as old as the Greek philosophers and the city-states they knew. Prince Clemens von Metternich, representing a nineteenth-century authoritarian state, said simply, "foreign affairs is not for the plebs." For much of the modern era the United States—distant from Europe's wars—was spared the most severe forms of this dilemma, but the European countries have known it well. The problem became acute after World War I, with full democratic franchises, the sacrifices the public had made in the war, and the delegitimation of the leadership as the result of those sacrifices and the outcome of the war.

British parliamentary democracy coexisted with an elitist and stratified social system; Britain's role as a major and sometimes dominant world power compelled a resolution of the debate in practice. Despite the success of popular pressures for appeasement in the 1930s, overall that practice was weighted fairly heavily away from direct popular control. Components of British practice included a system in which the prime minister usually could depend on a stable parliamentary majority and strong party discipline, a tradition of secrecy concerning cabinet deliberations, and a legal system with an Official Secrets Act that almost indefinitely prevented publication of a broad range of materials that had only tenuous connection to a reasonable definition of national security.

Lacking both the imperial experience and the overt social hierarchy of Britain, the United States had to face these issues squarely only in the twentieth century, and not in any sustained way until World War II and the subsequent cold war. World War II saw the birth of a large-scale national security bureaucracy, including the intelligence agencies, and the cold war the institution of a serious system of secrecy and classification of documents. The need for secrecy was driven in part by the assumption by the United States of the role of "imperial hegemon" of the Western alliance and the consequent worldwide entanglements, in part by the the reality of Soviet espionage and revelations about wartime treachery, and in part by the nature of modern weapons systems—nuclear weapons and the vehicles that carry them. Questions about the procurement, control, and possible use of nuclear weapons indeed pose the problem most starkly of all. Everyone has a stake, and therefore a "democratic" right to help decide about them, but the decision time would be so short and the results of using nuclear weapons would be so terrible that there is little room in which to tolerate error by those who are ignorant, stupid, or irrational.

National security issues in modern representative democracies are in many ways insulated from popular control and knowledge. There are the barriers of classification systems and protection of official secrets—a condition most acute in Israel, where the government does not even acknowledge the possession of nuclear weapons. Secrecy limits democracy both by restricting the material available to inform choices of policy, and by restricting the ability of the populace to inform itself on how well its policy preferences have been met. Another level of insulation derives from the assumption that strategic issues are extraordinarily complex and require a level of technical—often scientific—mastery beyond the capability of ordinary citizens. There is the language of strategists, full of arcane concepts and mysterious acronyms. These are often reinforced by the elites themselves; for example, among national security specialists no one who has failed to master the technical language is taken seriously. They consciously think they do indeed know best. They also find it convenient not to have to explain everything they do to a popular audience. Policymakers find it useful to cloak many of their actions in a veil of secrecy, sometimes in violation of the legalities of democratic procedure. An executive faced with a legislative majority that does not share the executive's perceptions of threat is tempted to resort to extralegal and secret procedures in defense of the "national interest" or even of its own partisan interest, as in the Iran-Contra affair.

At one level what Dahl (1985) calls the "democracy versus guardianship" debate seems to be over process and lofty principles, but that is deceptive. In the United States and most Western democracies the prevailing myth is closer to that of John Locke, the Founding Fathers, and Bastille Day than it is to Plato's guardians or Lenin's vanguard of the proletariat. Partisans rarely argue directly with the general principle of democratic control, but rather dispute whether the outcomes will be desirable in particular cases. Thus American liberal internationalists of the early post–World War II period were staunch promoters and defenders of democracy in general, but they distrusted the historic isolationist impulses of the American populace and feared that American democracy would not sustain the rigors of a long-term struggle against communist expansion. In this they shared Alexis de Tocqueville's concern (1945, esp. part I, chapter 13; first published 1835), more than a century earlier, about the ability of democracies to carry out stable policies and delicate, prolonged negotiations.

In contemporary debates, the division often seems to be between hawks and doves—however imperfect that distinction.

Doves often are found in, or leading, mass organizations to protest involvement in foreign conflicts (Vietnam, Central America) or to promote arms control and disarmament (the nuclear freeze movement). They try to stimulate broad public debate, and they applaud or promote graphic presentations of the horrors of nuclear war in the belief that repulsion from the horrors will lead also to repulsion from possession of nuclear weapons that could cause the horrors. Over the years, members of the left have insisted that a greater procedural commitment to popular rule, justifiable on grounds of democratic theory, would also produce substantively preferable policy outcomes. Hawks (and also many self-styled owls) castigate "fearmongering," try to reassure the populace that the government is following a responsible and informed course, worry about leaks of sensitive information to the public, and largely try to encapsulate any changes in policy within the bureaucracy rather than the public arena (again recall the Iran-Contra affair, exposed in 1986).

Many of these characteristics are nevertheless dependent on the elite consensus at the time, and advocacy of popular involvement may less reflect conviction about the democratic process than about the wisdom of particular policies and whether one is in or out of power. Doves worry about Rambo-like instincts among the mass public, and, as we have seen, hawks in the Reagan administration often effectively understood and enlisted popular support for their policies of an arms buildup and "negotiating from strength." Moreover, doves' faith that the people will be on their side is occasionally badly misinformed; note for example Adlai Stevenson's mishandling of the test-ban issue in the 1950s, or recent dovish misjudgments about the attractiveness of SDI to the public. If the mass public is sometimes ignorant about the details of national security issues, elites are sometimes equally ignorant about the basic hopes and fears that drive the attitudes of ordinary people.

Shared Responsibility

Any empirical analysis of public opinion risks being ephemeral. Specific policy questions and survey responses inevitably change. Many fundamental philosophical questions about the capacity of humans to govern themselves wisely are touched on only obliquely here. The most basic one, blending elements of fact and value, is what the nominal form of government shall be. That question has already been answered in the West (and increasingly in the East) with the word democracy. Democracy is considered to be better than the alternatives—faint praise, and an evaluation leaving open much about how deeply and broadly democratic control should reach. Many subsidiary questions do not yield well to confident generalizations. Few, however, have been shown here to offer grounds for the principled exclusion of popular voices from decisionmaking; that conclusion deserves not to be ephemeral.

If those who oppose a significant popular role in the formation of national security policy were correct, we should expect political systems with less popular involvement to show better policies—more adaptive for survival. Yet as we have seen, autocratic systems are losing place in the world, either being overthrown in favor of democratic governments or evolving in the direction of admitting broader popular participation. The motivating force behind much of this change is the inability of autocratic regimes to compete effectively in world politics (for example, contemporary Soviet experience). Moreover, when democracies and autocracies fight each other in war, democracies are significantly more likely to win (Lake, 1989). They are better information processors, and better able to motivate their citizens (Deutsch, 1963). As organisms adapted for survival, democracies in general are not doing at all badly. The findings of this book suggest some of the reasons.

In Chapter 2 we saw one of the most convincing examples to support the perspective that the populace is sometimes inappropriately bellicose: the rally 'round the flag phenomenon, frequently invoked by leaders interested as much in shoring up their domestic political position in the face of deteriorating economic conditions as in achieving particular foreign policy goals. The rally effect works most clearly for threats of military force or actual uses of force internationally, though it usually is discernible in response to decisive foreign policy action of any sort. American leaders seem especially likely to use or threaten force in the year before an election, although this relationship has been diluted by the "permanent referendum" of electronic media and opinion polls on the presidency during the past half-century.

In Israel, military actions against the Arabs have been more frequent in election years, and before the election more than afterward.

In general, leaders have been found to make less cognitively complex statements before elections, and lack of cognitive complexity in turn is associated with greater readiness to conduct military interventions and less readiness to conclude international agreements. Electoral pressures seem to encourage leaders to talk tough and act tough before elections, and to be most conciliatory toward foreign adversaries in middle years of their terms in office. The coincidence of certain kinds of international actions with the timing of the electoral cycle may make it difficult to conclude agreements with leaders of other states—democratic or otherwise—who must be responsive to the phases of their own domestic political systems.

This evidence of popular support for leaders who act belligerently in foreign affairs, support that may encourage such actions, enters the most important reservation in this book about the wisdom of democracies. It should nevertheless not be counted too heavily. Democracies in general are not more war-prone, nor more prone to use military force, than are nondemocratically governed states in similar roles of international power. The rally 'round the flag effect is very short-lived; after it the president's popularity returns to its previous level. Indeed, war itself is rarely popular. If a president has enmeshed his country in sustained fighting, his popularity, and that of his party, is likely to fall below its previous level, and he risks losing the next election. For Americans, the rally 'round the flag effect actually reflects the delegitimation of war in prospect as well as in retrospect; the rally is safely invoked only for action against terrorists, for international peacekeeping, to protect American citizens overseas, as with the hostages in Iran or the public justification for invading Grenada, or against small powers who cannot in turn threaten a long-drawn-out war or retaliation against the American heartland. The domestic political incentives to bellicosity are limited in duration and in the nature of their target.

Leaders of modern democracies lack traditional legitimation of their individual authority. In such states the leader's primary political task is to retain legitimacy by satisfying the material demands of constituents. But those demands, for an ever-improving condition, are hard to satisfy in any continuing manner in the real world of capitalist business cycles. The leader who cannot supply the material rewards which provide the rational legitimation of leadership must therefore grasp for charismatic leadership, perhaps by invoking the rally effect. Charismatic leadership, however, is ephemeral in a democratic culture whose materialism does not really admit the possibility of political heroes (as contrasted with cultural heroes of entertainment), and which retains the perceptiveness and rationality to punish the leader who does not deliver the material goods or who steps into long-term crisis or war. Rallying 'round the flag provides only a brief handhold for a tottering leader; imprudent reliance on it may later help push him over the precipice.

In Chapter 3 we found that different kinds of actions within a larger range of hypothetical ones can meet with public approval; leaders have some choice as to what actions to take, how to justify them, and how to assemble behind them a majority coalition. In a democracy, the most politically acceptable policies are those which combine elements of both sides of the political spectrum; people prefer acts that are both tough and open to negotiation; they want strength and peace. They are most supportive of arms agreements at times of relative security—when their fears of war are not too great, and when they see American arms as on a par with (not necessarily superior to) Russian ones.

Popular attitudes toward nuclear weapons show some ambivalence, but also an internal logic not necessarily inferior to that of many "experts." Most people have accepted the existential reality of nuclear deterrence, but lack enthusiasm for building specific new nuclear weapons systems. They are not sure whether the advent of nuclear weapons has raised or diminished the likelihood of war. Moreover, their attitudes toward nuclear weapons have shifted over the years; people have adjusted their thinking in accord with changing strategic realities. Notably, as the vulnerability of the Western alliance to Soviet nuclear retaliation has increased, so too have doubts about whether the invention of the bomb was "a good thing," opposition to building new weapons, and generalized opposition to the first use of nuclear weapons. Without learning to love the bomb, people have accepted the condition of nuclear parity with the Soviet Union and the condition of mutual deterrence.

They do not like the idea of first use of nuclear weapons because they assume, overwhelmingly, that any use of nuclear weapons will probably spiral out of control and cause immeasurable damage to their national heartland. War in general, and especially nuclear war, is not considered a legitimate policy. For ordinary people the notion of limited nuclear war is an oxymoron advocated by morons. Most people are not wedded to the principles of nuclear deterrence: they know deterrence is not defense, and they could accept a different kind of balance, especially one that truly emphasized defense. They are not, however, ready to renounce possession or first use of nuclear weapons unilaterally; as with the test ban, a majority is prepared to support only bilateral agreements.

Fears of war have fluctuated over time in response to international events and shifts in leaders' rhetoric, but they have almost always been highest in the United States, the leader and architect of the Western alliance. People's basic discomfort with nuclear weapons leaves them susceptible to utopian promises like SDI in the form of a leak-proof defensive shield, or to plans for drastic mutual nuclear disarmament by the superpowers. There is here a basic source of instability that can be harnessed by cynical leaders who would manipulate the public as well as by idealistic leaders who truly wish to make a dramatic break with the existing dilemmas of nuclear deterrence.

Potential support for disarmament and arms control agreements with the Soviet Union should not be confused with trust of Soviet intentions. Levels of distrust remain high, especially with a perception that Gorbachev may not be, or remain, reliably in control of Soviet policy. Agreements cannot be based on trust, but must depend on the ability to inspect and monitor Soviet compliance with the terms of the agreements. Suspicion of Soviet intentions has always been high, and was heightened by repeated official charges, in the first six years of the Reagan administration, that the Soviets always lie, cheat, and violate agreements. The administration first outflanked proponents of a nuclear freeze with the promise of the SDI shield, and then decimated their forces with the allegations that the Soviet Union had violated virtually all previous arms control accords. In so doing the administration neatly adapted both elements of a "peace through strength" advocacy to a line more subtle than its previous concentration just on a huge military buildup. Doves would do well to study that process.

Any American president who concludes with the Soviet Union an agreement which lacks persuasive evidence of verification brings trouble on himself. If a treaty, it may be rejected by the Senate, or passed only after the president has paid a disproportionate political price in concessions to placate the skeptics. If ratified, or if it is an agreement that does not require ratification, it will remain hostage to charges by hawkish opponents that the Soviets have not abided by it. Whatever the technical merits of inspection as judged by national security specialists, a lack of provisions for inspection that allay public fears guarantees political discord.

Chapter 3 also provided further evidence for the "centrist" nature and the suspicion of "extremes" which characterize most popular opinion on security policy. The great bulk of the population is not isolationist, nor extremely hawkish, nor pacifist. A president is rewarded for showing that he is within this centrist mainstream; that is, his popularity rises when he acts more dovish than his hawkish reputation would suggest, and vice versa. Candidates for national office must avoid being identified as too close to either end of the spectrum, as Barry Goldwater was perhaps unjustly identified in 1964. The British Labour party, with its unilateralist disarmament stance in the June 1983 elections, almost surely paid the price of going beyond the bounds of political prudence. Some advisers have urged the Democrats to develop a "right hook" on security policy to go with the "left jab" of domestic policy. That's the kind of advice that put Michael Dukakis in a tank. Better advice would be: study the champs, bob and weave a little, hit the heart as well as the head, but don't swing wildly.

The center, of course, is always defined according to the range of policies deemed at least vaguely within the bounds of responsible discussion. Both surrender and genocide of the adversary nation, for example, are beyond those bounds in peacetime—but either can become more respectable under certain wartime conditions. The center of American opinion on security issues has shifted somewhat over the years, not only in attitudes toward nuclear weaponry but in attitudes toward the principal adversaries. Orientations toward China underwent a sea change in the 1970s and 1980s. Recently there has emerged a greater willingness to undertake cooperative problem-solving with the Soviet Union, and better overall feelings toward the Soviet Union. In these shifts the populace has responded to changes in Soviet actions and in both Soviet and American rhetoric; they could shift back again if the actions and rhetoric shift. Movement in this "center"—which comprises the majority of the American population—is possible, and only partially under the control of American governmental leaders.

Chapter 4 carried on this question of how government and the public interact. We found that the public was generally not well informed about the details of nuclear weaponry and strategy—though they know more about armaments than about arms control—but that the people are fairly interested in the topic at times when most informed observers would agree that it should matter most. Public opinion on most issues is reasonably stable, not capricious, fickle, or volatile. On those matters for which substantial change over time can be identified—China, the Soviet Union, or the proper level of defense spending—attitudes seem to respond to real changes in world conditions. When defense spending has been high for a while and the Soviet Union's behavior has been relatively pacific, people are ready to cut military spending; when the opposite conditions are true, they are ready to increase it.

Government policy and public opinion do interact. Government leaders try to lead opinion in desired directions, but often have to settle for choosing, from a broad menu of possible actions, those which are likely to be sustained by public opinion. This is true for the detailed execution of policy as well as for setting the broad outlines, and governments spend much energy and resources in determining what kinds of policies will be acceptable. The pressures to discern what will be acceptable, in act and in verbal "framing," have grown as the ability to survey public opinion promptly and reliably has grown.

Broad-gauged popular belief systems (as well as attitudes on specific issues) are quite stable, and are structured and organized in a reasonably coherent manner. The structure is not so complex or coherent for members of the mass public as for the elites, but it is substantial and not to be dismissed simply because it may not always correspond precisely to the structure of elite opinion. If government policy (as on defense spending, or how to deal with the Russians) sometimes flip-flops, the flip-flops are not properly attributable to public volatility. Mass and elite opinions are not readily reducible to a single dimension of sentiment or policy. This multidimensionality of opinion, at both mass and elite levels, is the primary cause of changes in policy, as the coalitions supporting particular policies inevitably shift. These changes can be frustrating to friends and adversaries alike, but also serve to prevent the long-term ascendancy of any extreme and the consequent alienation of large numbers of people from the political system.

In Chapter 5 we established that while democracies are not especially peaceful in general, they rarely fight one another. In addition, we found evidence, both from a centuries-long perspective and on a fifteen-year time horizon, that democratic ideology and practice are becoming more common in the world; more states can accurately be characterized as democracies in the Western meaning of that term, and many others have at least shifted in the direction of greater observance of democratic principles. The public in Western democracies is aware of these shifts, including those in the USSR; conceivably, despite continuing suspicion of the Soviet government and its intentions, greater trust of the Soviet Union will ensue. Improved facilities for monitoring human rights policies, and greater flow of information between East and West, will help increase popular acceptance of the Soviet Union as a combination of partner and adversary rather than as a wholly hostile enemy. Changes in domestic and foreign policy in the Soviet Union, reinforced by appropriate international action to monitor and strengthen those changes, thus provide a chance for a significantly less belligerent policy by the United States, ultimately leading to a better capacity to avoid military confrontations and to dampen the severity of what crises do occur.

Elitist critics of *homo politicus* (female and male) have perpetuated various myths about that creature. We have, however, here seen evidence to debunk many of those myths. Specifically, we reject the following propositions:

1. That in democratic politics, as currently constrained by secrecy and the claims of expertise, security policy is free of considerations of partisan or private interest. Much evidence, especially that about elites' manipulation of the rally 'round the flag effect, tells us otherwise.

2. That *homo democraticus* is prone to extremes, either of aggressiveness or passivity, that would consistently shift security policy away from some prudent balance of the two. On the contrary, *homo democraticus* is largely centrist, and is an essential element of the balancing mechanism.

3. That *homo democraticus* is fickle and easily manipulated: at best politically irrelevant (and best kept that way), and at worst politically incapable of supporting a consistent security policy. Rather, public opinion is quite stable, often advocates or supports policy change that makes "rational" sense in international affairs, and in the long run is often effective in getting its way.

4. That *homo democraticus* is, in an anarchic world, ethnocentric and constantly "at war" with all other peoples. Rather, while popular ethnocentrism sometimes approves violent actions, an element of that ethnocentrism can promote good relations with states seen as governed by similarly "democratic" regimes. Those who partake of democratic culture are more nearly in a state of perceptual peace with other democratic peoples.

Removal of these myths provides the basis for a clearer understanding of the potential for as well as the constraints on achieving and sustaining a security policy in the common interest. I do not imagine that the detailed choice and execution of security policy can be conducted by referendum, or without extended deliberation, or lacking the consideration of technical experts, or entirely in the public eye. Levels of information in the mass public are not high; the person in the street can rarely be depended on to make a complex and reliable judgment about the merits of a particular weapons system or a particular arms control verification procedure. But information levels are quite adequate to set basic and stable principles to guide public policy. These principles are heavily concerned with normative judgments as well as with empirical facts, and they are not trivial. When is the use of military force justified? Should we seek military superiority over the Soviets, or should we settle for parity? Are our military defense levels basically adequate, or seriously wanting? How important is it to have a modus vivendi with the Soviets? What risks are we prepared to run to avoid being red? or dead?

These partly normative questions are ones to which people can provide some answers—not always well articulated, but considered, sincere, and reasonably consistent over time.[1] They are parameters for policy, and certainly not meaningless. And most people are not, by the standards of most experts, extreme in their judgments. Most of the propositions summarized here seem to apply, with some modifications for particular circumstances, to most Western democracies. The security policy of Western democracies may well be wrong in the sense that it cannot produce over the long run the kind of stable and peaceful world to which we aspire. But if so, "the people" are not so markedly discontent with that policy that one would anticipate sharp changes if somehow the people were to acquire a much larger voice in the determination of policy. Elites and mass must share responsibility for where we are and what we have become. The right question is how both can achieve changes in policy where appropriate.

Nuclear Command and Control

Two issues illustrate some key elements of the problem of achieving change. The first—problems of nuclear command and control—is essentially one of how in the near future to remove some grievous flaws in the present posture of deterrence so as to make it more stable. The second is whether, and how, a long-term change in the basic nature of the Soviet-American confrontation may occur so as to lessen the reliance on nuclear deterrence.

Over the past few years many experts have written powerful critiques of the command, control, communication, and intelligence (C^3I) facilities for nuclear weapons (e.g., Blair, 1985;

---

1. Americans believe they *ought* to have a voice, overwhelmingly agreeing that "the issue of nuclear war is too important to leave only to the President and the experts," and rejecting the proposition that it "is too complex for people like me to think about." *Americans Talk Security*, 1987, p. 306.

Bracken, 1984). Their arguments are largely persuasive to many defense specialists across the political spectrum. They contend that whereas the vulnerability of strategic nuclear weapons themselves has been exaggerated, C³I has been vulnerable to Soviet attack at least since the early 1970s, with the result that American strategic nuclear retaliatory capability has been unreliable in two senses. First—the continuing nightmare of the doves—is the risk that in a crisis, faced with ambiguous information about an apparent Soviet attack and the knowledge that the C³I capability to conduct any substantial controlled response may not survive after that capability has been hit, the National Command Authority (NCA) will authorize a large-scale "retaliatory" nuclear strike under circumstances when the apparent attack is not in fact occurring or when the attack is so ragged or minimal as not to deserve such a response. The second sense relates to the stereotypical nightmare of the hawk—that the NCA will quickly lose the ability to retaliate, and will lack the will to do so during the short period while it is still able; and that, seeing this, the Soviet Union will be emboldened to attack during a political-military confrontation.

The experts' fears reflect an extreme degree of alienation of the execution of national security policy from both the mass and the elites. No one, outside of a very narrow circle of military officers, would affect decisions for survival or vengeance. In part the two fears (those of the hawks and of the doves) reflect a real dilemma between tight control that would prevent mistaken launching and looser control that would facilitate correctly informed launching, but in large part both concerns could be addressed by similar improvements in organization and technology. It follows that there should be convergence, across the political spectrum, on the need to strengthen C³I and restore some semblance of control, if not by the mass public at least in a form delegated to their elected representatives.

Yet whereas deficiencies in C³I have been well recognized in the community of defense intellectuals for many years, no adequate steps have been taken to correct them. Public discussions of deterrence and arms control have overwhelmingly focused on the traditional dimensions of weapons numbers and capabilities. Arms control agreements, proposed and concluded, have concentrated on bean counting; presidential election campaigns have

been hardly more subtle than as to whether the candidate favors
or opposes a strong defense. Minimal effort has been made to
create a public constituency for debate on C³I, and actions within
the government to shift resources to improving C³I have been
insubstantial. At best, improvements have only kept pace with
increases in the number and complexity of Soviet and American
weapons systems, producing no net improvement (Blair, 1985).
To what degree may this profound misallocation of attention be
rooted in the nature of democratic politics?

Surely the reasons for the neglect are complex, and many of
them are tangential to the subject of this book. They include
problems of organizational behavior and bureaucratic politics.
C³I is the responsibility of no particular service. Hence, no service will fight political battles for it, and the services will even
resist increases in budgetary allocation for C³I if the increases
will endanger allocations for weapons. C³I is largely in the
domain of professional military officers; an effort to assert
greater control by the president and other members of the NCA
would raise divisive issues of civil-military relations. To confront C³I problems seriously would also require the president
and his staff to confront fears of their own personal vulnerability.
If C³I is vulnerable, they will be the first to die in a nuclear war.
Thinking about this prospect requires overcoming powerful psychological defense mechanisms against thinking about one's
own death. Overall, the elites have lacked incentive to do something serious about the problem, despite its obvious importance
to the national interest.

In addition, fixing C³I will be expensive, requiring public support and a public willingness to spend large sums of money. As
we have seen, most of the time the general public does not favor
spending more for defense, except for periods when Soviet-American relations have markedly deteriorated and/or when a reasonable case can be made that the United States is in danger of
falling behind in important elements of the military balance.
Neither of those conditions has applied in recent years. Thus
professional politicians will be reluctant to advocate sharply
enhanced funding for C³I. Moreover, C³I has little political constituency. It is not part of the way in which strategic issues have
been framed in the public debate, and hence there is no ready-

made popular demand for it, as there may be for arms reduction or arms increases.

Raising the C³I issue in public discussion raises individuals' fears there too. Improving C³I is associated, both for the public and for the strategic community, with strategies for fighting limited nuclear war. Indeed, many of the measures needed to diminish the problems of C³I could also have the effect of making limited nuclear war seem more feasible. But limited nuclear war is not a politically popular concept, since most people believe that any use of nuclear weapons would inevitably escalate to all-out nuclear war. During the first two years of the Reagan administration talk about limited nuclear war proved politically counterproductive, and had to be cut back. Similarly, the Kennedy administration's advocacy of backyard fallout shelters was widely resisted, and eventually abandoned because it made the specter of nuclear war more imminent without convincing people that it would significantly improve their prospects for survival.

An acceptable public case for improvement of C³I will require a more complex and nuanced presentation than has usually been feasible in discussions of strategic issues. Perhaps it is more amenable to a political "fix" than to technological ones. For example, Blair (1985, pp. 289–295) has suggested that strategic stability would be strengthened, in combination with technical improvements, by the adoption of a policy of "no immediate second strike." That is, the NCA would adopt, and be technically enabled to implement, a policy of retaliation only after twenty-four hours or so had elapsed following any single-wave impact of an adversary's weapons on the United States. With both weapons and C³I suited to a secure second-strike posture, retaliation might become more certain at the same time as crisis stability was strengthened. Some aspects of this policy would undoubtedly be popular—as manifested, for example, in the existing support for no first use. Other aspects—such as the intent to defer vengeance—would not be so certain of popular acquiescence. As on other issues, public preferences for toughness, conciliation, and avoidance of war all need to be considered together. The potential to frame this issue as nonextremist, addressing fears of both hawks and doves, can be drawn upon.

Basic concepts about survivable and nonprovocative retaliatory forces (second-strike-only weapons) are still not well understood among the general public—nor even in Congress.[2] National security elites discuss these problems all the time among themselves, but efforts to explain them to a wider audience have been inadequate. Certainly they are difficult concepts to grasp. Yet the elites themselves are ambivalent, and therefore in no hurry to expand the discussion. It is easy enough to favor second-strike-only weapons as a means of stabilizing Soviet-American deterrence in times of crisis and mutual fears of surprise attack. But there is an inherent contradiction between limiting oneself to second-strike weapons and the still-customary policy of threatening to use nuclear weapons first in the event of a Soviet invasion of Western Europe that seemed about to succeed. Whereas the credibility of that threat has demonstrably eroded over the past decades, most Western policymakers are reluctant to abandon it entirely, either in declaratory policy or in the force postures that might conceivably make it viable. Without some elite consensus on whether to try to make a first-use policy viable with first-strike weapons, or to abandon both—and then to explain that resolution as sensible policy—it is hardly surprising that the public only poorly comprehends the issues.

Democracies do not make war on one another because the people—those in the streets, not just elites—understand that military force is irrelevant to settling disputes between governments which rest on free consent rather than on force. That understanding is of a simple yet subtle proposition. The proposition that nuclear weapons have no utility in war is similarly simple yet subtle, and reasonably well understood by the public. Translating it into public policy is an enormously complex task, but assertions about public ignorance, volatility, or lack of interest are just not accurate. The C^3I issue illustrates a problem of national and international security that demands sophisticated public attention. The elites have not satisfactorily dealt with it; it is a fundamental subject for democratic governance.

---

2. Congressman Thomas Downey (1984, p. 458) reports that after his unsuccessful opposition to the Trident II missile, a friendly Armed Services Committee staff member asked, "Tom, why are you wasting your time with that destabilizing crap? If you wanted to win your amendment, you should have talked about cost."

The Future of Soviet-American Relations

Technological solutions to the dangers of superpower rivalry in the nuclear era—whether those solutions be securely stabilizing the C^3I problem or visionary ones such as an impenetrable SDI—are not promising. The technology is at best distantly available, and under the best of circumstances will require political innovation as well. Perhaps a continuation of something like the current strategic balance, at a reduced level of weaponry, is the most we can reasonably hope for. Many people—experts and mass public alike—seem to think so, and take comfort in the fact that war between the superpowers has already been avoided for such a long time. But many experts are not at all comfortable with such a confrontation, measured in decades or centuries. Nor is much of the general public, as evidenced by their ambivalence about nuclear weapons and first use, and by their susceptibility to "radical" solutions like SDI (but not to other radical solutions like unilateral disarmament or preventive war). The inherent dilemmas of nuclear strategy also demand a long-term change in Soviet-American relations, one that cannot realistically be expected to prevent all superpower crises, but one that can make them less likely to spiral into war.

Public attraction to SDI is distinguished by the fact that, whereas it may be a radical notion in the sense of being outside the predominant expert consensus during most of the cold war era, it is not easily placeable near the extremes of any simple "hawk-dove" spectrum. Members of the elite may largely divide that way on the issue, but approval of SDI among the general public is poorly related to hawk-dove characterizations or other foreign policy divisions. On issues that do fit hawk-dove or internationalist-interventionist spectra the public remains, as we have seen, pretty "centrist" in resisting the siren calls of radical change.

We may liken this centrism, or the politics of opposites, to a kind of homeostatic thermostat to avoid temperature extremes. When the house is too warm, the thermostat cuts off the heat, and when the house is too cold it turns it on. But acceptance of that image overlooks the fact that the equilibrium point of the thermostat may vary under different circumstances. Within certain obvious biological limits, people can learn to tolerate, and even to like, rather different temperatures. An Eskimo, a German, and a Sudanese would initially set the thermostat at different levels, but over long years of living in the same culture and climate they might converge in their preferences, and even that convergence point would probably shift in response to drastic changes in the cost of heating or cooling. In other words, the center is not immutable, nor is the range. People may become willing to let the house warm up beyond the level at which the thermostat is set. Their preferences change in response to external conditions, including perceived costs and opportunities.

A combination of the "politics of opposites" with the phenomenon of shifting coalitions across dimensions insures that there will be changes of policy. Changes will occur in the composition of elite coalitions and, insofar as the general public thinks foreign policy is important, in the mass coalitions on which the elite ones are based. There is some potential for a drastic change in the political equilibrium; the image of a thermostat should not be taken too literally. Nevertheless, it is not likely that a coalition based near the extremes of the system can attain or hold power for long. Both Goldwater and George McGovern were perceived as "extremists" on foreign as well as domestic policy, and were soundly defeated. Ronald Reagan was first elected by a bare majority of popular votes, and the composition of his initial foreign and security policy staff was untypical of mass or elite opinion as represented at the end of Chapter 4; that is, it was concentrated more in the "hard-liner" quadrant. Policy in his first term probably departed more from the post–World War II "mainstream" than did that of any previous administration. But by the second term it shifted back much more into that mainstream, perhaps having moved the center some but not drastically.

The often centripetal effects of democratic politics may not always be benign. The United States has been blessed by its geographical isolation and its relative immunity from military conquest. A political system facing chronic, intense, and difficult-to-resolve problems of national security, however, can be hamstrung, unable to move significantly in any constructive direction. In Israel, for example, no government seems able to move effectively either toward a trade of territory and Arab self-determination for peace or toward territorial annexation and explusion of the Arab population. Expulsion is still morally unacceptable to the majority of Israeli Jews, and any move to surrender much territory is subject to blocking not only by majority vote but by the institutionalized resistance of a religious minority and especially by the Jewish settlers in the occupied territories. The centrist compromise thus becomes resignation to a status quo which may not be sustainable in the long term. Is a "centrist" American commitment to indefinite nuclear deterrence forever sustainable in a world of evolving technology, changing ideologies, and shifting power?

Under the best of circumstances, long-term and substantial shifts in the center of any democratic system can be achieved only with a balanced effort. Any political leader who wishes to move in a more "idealistic" direction will have to incorporate some basic realist principles: of strength, skepticism, recognition of the continuing existence of serious rivalries and conflicts of interest among nation-states, and demand for reciprocation of conciliatory acts. Both rhetoric and action must pay deference to these principles; otherwise the effort courts political disaster at home as well as abroad.

Attitudes toward the Soviet Union are among those which can change over time, in response both to political leadership and to change in international realities. After all, the American public was originally persuaded of the need to defend the Free World against the Soviet threat very soon after World War II in which the predominant image of the Soviet Union had been that of a determined ally against Nazi Germany. Similarly, attitudes toward Germany and Japan shifted from foe to friend in only a slightly longer timespan. It is not too much to hope that attitudes toward the Soviet Union will continue to become more favorable, providing that Soviet behavior continues on a moderate path. Because most Westerners' attitudes toward the Soviet Union are founded in very little concrete information, new pieces of information have the potential to make a great difference. Attitudinal change in the West is being helped by information about the current Soviet leaders' movement away from the standard Bolshevik principles of centralized economic and political control.

Members of the general public do have very distinct images of other countries, not simply undifferentiated views of all outsiders or foreigners. It is thus appropriate to think about the relations between pairs of countries, such as the United States and the Soviet Union, and their particular characteristics. People can readily, and predictably, discriminate between states they see as friendly and others. Among Americans, positive images of other countries are closely associated with two characteristics of those countries: the degree of American interest manifested in them (measured by trade, investment, and military ties) and the degree to which they are culturally similar to the United States (including race, religion, language, political system, and income level: see Nincic and Russett, 1979).[3] The importance of form of government to Americans' liking of other countries is evident in a 1986 survey (Reilly, 1987). Of the ten countries toward which feelings were warmest, all but two were democracies and the exceptions only partly nondemocratic (Mexico, fifth, and Brazil, tenth). Of the lowest thirteen, all but two were clearly not democracies (exceptions being India, seventeenth, and Nigeria, nineteenth).

Of the various elements above, ties of military alliance are hardly relevant. The Soviet Union and the United States will never be close trading partners, owing to the substantial degree of self-sufficiency each possesses. But there is much potential for more commercial exchange than currently exists. Their economies have great complementarities, with the American comparative advantage in agricultural production and high-technology goods and the Soviet reserves of many natural resources. Cultural similarity, moderately high on some worldwide scale, may be strengthened by the kinds of economic and political changes currently in progress in the USSR. By none of these criteria can we expect a truly warm relationship, but further thaw does not seem too much to hope for.

Past rivalries between major powers have often turned into relationships of stable peace; for example, Britain and the United States or Britain and France (Rock, 1989). More important, there

3. That this is not purely a dimension picking up ties to Europe is evidenced by the high ranking of Japan even as early as 1976, above France and near Germany and Italy among countries toward which Americans felt favorably. Informal inspection of Europeans' attitudes toward other countries (*Eurobarometre*, 1986, pp. 35–42) suggests similar determinants as for Americans.

are historical precedents for the mutation of even such an intense and ideologically driven rivalry as the Soviet-American one. Most notable is the Treaty of Westphalia in 1648, marking the end of the vicious Thirty Years War between the Catholics and Protestants of Europe. In that treaty the rulers reaffirmed the legitimacy of one another's regimes on the principle of national self-determination. Or, more precisely, the principle was of the ruler's self-determination: *cuius regio, eius religio*; the king's religion shall be the people's. Europeans fought great wars thereafter, but not along the great faultlines of religion, and whereas the religious differences remained, most of them lost their political relevance and ultimately even their ideological fervor. Furthermore, until the twentieth century these nonreligious wars were usually more limited and less destructive than were those driven by religious ideology. (The Napoleonic wars, impelled by a different ideological split, are the major exception.)

There are two important differences, and one similarity, between the seventeenth-century basis of coexistence and the possiblity of such an arrangement between the United States and the Soviet Union today. One difference is that the Westphalian settlement came only after hideous warfare. A hoped-for solution that envisages Soviet-American "coexistence" of a sort only after a thermonuclear war is hardly a hopeful prospect. In contemporary circumstances, the anticipation of what might happen if the rivalry is unchecked must substitute for the actual experience of it. Popular understanding of what nuclear weapons can do suggests this may be a reasonable substitution. A second difference is that the seventeenth-century solution really was an arrangement between rulers, without regard to how they treated their subjects. It was less a guarantee that rulers could enforce their religious preferences on their subjects (often they could not), however, than an affirmation of the principle of nonintervention by other rulers. A late-twentieth-century analogue would include the latter, while explicitly incorporating the principle of observing basic human rights as the foundation for popular perceptions of mutual legitimacy.

The important similarity is that the Westphalian settlement did not depend upon the former adversaries' uniting against some common rival. Peace was born from exhaustion rather than from

a perception of Turkey or other Moslem states as serious enemies—a threat that had palpably been declining before 1648.
The Soviet Union and the United States do not today have any
major common political adversary. American relations with
China have been relatively normal for some time, and Soviet-
Chinese relations are now warming as well. Cooperation
between two powers does not always depend upon the syndrome
of "the enemy of my enemy is my friend." The improvement in
Soviet-American relations in the 1970s (however temporary)
happened simultaneously with the strengthening of Sino-Amer-
ican relations, at both the level of governmental action and that
of popular attitudes. Leaders on all sides of the triangle tried to
play off the others' rivalries, but progress in one relationship did
not depend on deterioration in the other. Over the years,
improvements in American-Soviet and American-Chinese relations have tended to occur together—though until recently these
improvements were associated with greater Soviet-Chinese hostility (Freeman and Goldstein, 1989).

  If there is a common threat faced by the United States and the
Soviet Union today—and by all other countries—it is from the
decay of the environment, particularly the dangers of climatic
change from global warming and ozone depletion. Cooperation
against this kind of common adversary will not be easy; conflicting national interests remain, and a statement of hope risks
sounding merely trendy. Nonetheless, such cooperation would
present the possibility of peaceful joint action, and could provide
an experience of common problem-solving that might spill over
into more politically sensitive arenas. Asked in 1988 to evaluate
threats to national security over the next five years, 77 percent
of Americans labeled global environmental threats as serious or
very serious; only 50 percent so characterized an "increase in
Soviet military strength" (Martilla, 1989, p. 266).

  From some combination of realist and idealist perspectives
there is reason for optimism about the future of Soviet-American
relations and the chances for a more peaceful world. Those
chances do not require further insulation between the elite politics of government-to-government relations and the mass politics which give a government its legitimacy and stability. To the
contrary, popular attitudes in democratic countries share most
of the essential perspectives common among the elites, includ-

ing a mixture of idealism and practical realism. Elites who wish to lead their peoples along more cooperative international paths will find a favorable public response to carefully prepared arguments. Indeed, perhaps the leaders can be led in that direction by their peoples.

References

Abelson, Robert P. 1964. Mathematical models of the distribution of attitudes under controversy. In *Contributions to Mathematical Psychology*, ed. Norman Frederiksen and Harold Gulliksen. New York: Holt, Rinehart.

—— 1979. Social clusters and opinion clusters. In *Perspectives on Social Network Research*, ed. P. W. Holland and S. Leinhardt. New York: Academic Press.

Abramowitz, Alan, David Lanoue, and Subrha Ramesh. 1988. Economic conditions, causal attributions, and political evaluations in the 1984 presidential election. *Journal of Politics* 50(4): 848–863.

Abravanel, Martin, and Barry Hughes. 1975. Public attitudes and foreign policy behavior in Western democracies. In *The Analysis of Foreign Policy Outputs*, ed. William Chittick. Columbus, Oh.: Charles Merrill.

Achen, Christopher. 1975. Mass political attitudes and the survey response. *American Political Science Review* 69(4): 1218–1231.

—— 1978. Measuring representation. *Public Opinion Quarterly* 42: 455–510.

—— 1983. Toward theories of data: The state of political methodology. In *Political Science: The State of the Discipline*, ed. Ada W. Finifter. Washington, D.C.: American Political Science Association.

Adler, Kenneth. 1986. West European and American public opinion on peace, defence, and arms control in a cross-national perspective. *International Social Science Journal* 38(4): 589–600.

Aldrich, John, John Sullivan, and Eugene Borgida. 1989. Foreign affairs and issue voting: do presidential candidates "waltz before a blind audience"? *American Political Science Review* 83(1): 123–141.

Allison, Graham. 1970–71. Cool it: The foreign policy of young America. *Foreign Policy* 1: 144–60.

Almond, Gabriel. 1950. *The American People and Foreign Policy*. New Haven: Yale University Press.

Alt, James E., and K. Alec Chrystal. 1983. *Political Economy.* Berkeley: University of California Press.

Americans Talk Security. 1987. *Compendium of Poll Findings on the National Security Issue.* New York: Daniel Yankelovich Group.

―――― 1988–89. National Survey Reports, various monthly issues. New York: Daniel Yankelovich Group; Boston: Martilla and Kiley.

Anderson, Jack. 1988. White House took polls to make sure public would back bombing of Libya. *New Haven Register,* February 28, B3.

Arendt, Hannah. 1952. *Imperialism.* Part 2 of *The Origins of Totalitarianism.* New York: Harcourt Brace.

Arian, Asher. 1977. *Israel Election Study, 1973: Findings.* Tel Aviv: Tel Aviv University, Political Science Department.

―――― 1985. *Israeli Opinion and the War in Lebanon.* Tel Aviv: Tel Aviv University, Jaffee Center for Strategic Studies.

Arian, Asher, Tamar Herman, and Ilan Talmud. 1988. *National Security Policy and Public Opinion in Israel: The Guardian of Israel.* Boulder, Colo.: Westview.

Arian, Asher et al. 1989. *National Security and Public Opinion.* Tel Aviv: Tel Aviv University, Jaffee Center for Strategic Studies.

Ashley, Richard K. 1980. *The Political Economy of War and Peace.* London: Frances Pinter.

Barzilai, Gad, and Bruce Russett. 1990. The political economy of Israeli military action. In *The Elections in Israel—1988,* ed. Asher Arian and Michal Shamir. Boulder, Colo.: Westview.

Beal, Richard S., and Ronald H. Hinckley. 1984. Presidential decisionmaking and opinion polls. *Annals of the American Academy of Social Science: Polling and the democratic consensus* 472: 72–84.

Beck, Nathaniel. 1984. Domestic political sources of American monetary policy, 1955–82. *Journal of Politics* 46(3): 786–817.

Beitz, Charles R. 1979. *Political Theory and International Relations.* Princeton, N.J.: Princeton University Press.

Ben-Hanen, Uriel, and Benny Temkin. 1986. The overloaded juggler: The electoral economic cycle in Israel. In *The Elections in Israel—1984,* ed. Asher Arian and Michal Shamir. New Brunswick, N.J.: Transaction.

Benson, John M. 1982. The polls: U.S. military intervention. *Public Opinion Quarterly* 46: 592–598.

Bernstein, Barton. 1987. A postwar myth: 500,000 U.S. lives saved. *Bulletin of the Atomic Scientists* 42(6): 38–40.

Bernstein, Richard J. 1983. *Beyond Objectivism and Relativism.* Philadelphia: University of Pennsylvania Press.

Betts, Richard. 1987. *Nuclear Blackmail and Nuclear Balance.* Washington, D.C.: Brookings Institution.

Beyme, Klaus von. 1987. *America as a Model: The Impact of Democracy in the World.* Aldershot, Hampshire: Gower.

Blainey, Geoffrey. 1973. *The Causes of War.* New York: Free Press.

Blair, Bruce. 1985. *Strategic Command and Control.* Washington, D.C.: Brookings Institution.

Bloom, H. S., and H. Douglas Price. 1975. Voter response to short-run economic conditions: The asymmetrical effect of prosperity and recession. *American Political Science Review* 69(4): 1240–1254.

Bobrow, Davis. 1969. The organization of American national security opinions. *Public Opinion Quarterly* 33(1): 221–239.

———— 1989. Japan in the world: Opinion from defeat to success. *Journal of Conflict Resolution* 33(4): 571–603.

Boudreau, Thomas E. 1984. *The Secretary General and Satellite Diplomacy.* New York: Council on Religion and International Affairs.

Boulding, Kenneth E. 1979. *Stable Peace.* Austin: University of Texas Press.

Boyer, Paul. 1985. *By the Bomb's Early Light: American Thought and Culture at the Dawn of the Atomic Age.* New York: Pantheon.

Boyle, Francis Anthony. 1985. *World Politics and International Law.* Durham, N.C.: Duke University Press.

Bracken, Paul. 1984. *The Command and Control of Nuclear Forces.* New Haven, Conn.: Yale University Press.

———— 1988. Do we really want to eliminate the chances of accidental war? *Defense Analysis* 4(1): 81–90.

Brandt, Willi. 1980. *North-South: A Program for Survival.* Cambridge, Mass.: M.I.T. Press.

Brody, Richard. 1984. International crises: A rallying point for the president? *Public Opinion* 6: 41–43, 46.

Brody, Richard, and Benjamin Page. 1975. The impact of events on presidential popularity: The Johnson and Nixon administrations. In *Perspectives on the Presidency,* ed. Aaron Wildavsky. Boston: Little, Brown.

Brody, Richard, and Catherine Shapiro. 1987. Policy failure and public support: Reykjavik, Iran and public assessments of President Reagan. Paper presented at the annual meeting of the American Political Science Association, Chicago.

Brown, T. A., and Arthur A. Stein. 1982. The political economy of national elections. *Comparative Politics* 14(4): 479–497.

Bryen, Shoshana. 1980. That was the war that was. *Public Opinion* 3: 10–11, 58.

Bundy, McGeorge, George Kennan, Robert McNamara, and Gerard Smith. 1982. Nuclear weapons and the Atlantic Alliance. *Foreign Affairs* 60(4): 753–768.

Cantril, Albert H., ed. 1980. *Polling on the Issues.* Washington, D.C.: Seven Locks Press.

Cantril, Hadley. 1967. *The Human Dimension: Experiences in Policy Research.* New Brunswick, N.J.: Rutgers University Press.

Capitanchik, David, and Richard Eichenberg. 1983. *Defence and Public Opinion.* London: Routledge and Kegan Paul.

Carr, William. 1972. *Arms, Autarky and Aggression: A Study in German Foreign Policy, 1933–1939.* London: Camelot.

Caspary, William. 1970. The mood theory: A study of public opinion and foreign policy. *American Political Science Review* 64: 536–547.

Chan, Steve. 1984. Mirror, mirror on the wall . . . are the freer countries more pacific? *Journal of Conflict Resolution* 28(4): 617–648.

Choucri, Nazli, and Robert C. North. 1975. *Nations in Conflict.* New York: W. H. Freeman.

Cohen, Bernard C. 1973. *The Public's Impact on Foreign Policy.* Boston: Little, Brown.

Condorcet, Nicholas Caritat de. 1785. *Essai sur l'application de l'analyse à la probabilité des decisions rendues à la pluralité de voix.* Paris.

Converse, Philip. 1964. The nature of belief systems in mass publics. In *Ideology and Discontent,* ed. David Apter. New York: Free Press.

Cotton, Timothy Y. C. 1986. War and American democracy: Voting trends in the last five American wars. *Journal of Conflict Resolution* 30(4): 616–635.

Craig, Gordon A., and Alexander George. 1983. *Force and Statecraft: Diplomatic Problems of Our Time.* New York: Oxford University Press.

Crespi, Irving. 1980. The case of presidential popularity. In *Polling on the Issues,* ed. Albert H. Cantril. Washington, D.C.: Seven Locks Press.

Cusack, Thomas R. 1989. On the domestic political-economic sources of military spending. Paper presented at the annual meeting of the American Political Science Association, Atlanta.

Dahl, Robert A. 1971. *Polyarchy: Participation and Opposition.* New Haven, Conn.: Yale University Press.

——— 1985. *Controlling Nuclear Weapons: Democracy versus Guardianship.* Syracuse: Syracuse University Press.

——— 1988. Democracy and human rights under different conditions of development. Paper prepared for the Nobel Symposium on Human Rights, Oslo.

de Boer, Connie. 1981. The polls: Our commitment to World War III. *Public Opinion Quarterly* 45(1): 126–134.

——— 1984. The polls: The European peace movement and deployment of nuclear missiles. *Public Opinion Quarterly* 49(1): 119–132.

den Oudsten, Eymert. 1986. Public opinion on peace and war. In Stockholm International Peace Research Institute, *World Armaments and Disarmament: SIPRI Yearbook 1986.* Oxford: Oxford University Press.

——— 1988. Public opinion on international security: A comparative study of the Federal Republic of Germany, the Netherlands, the United Kingdom, and the United States, 1979–87. Master's thesis, Groningen University, Sociology Department.

Destler, Irving, Leslie Gelb, and Anthony Lake. 1984. *Our Own Worst Enemy: The Unmaking of American Foreign Policy.* New York: Simon and Schuster.

Deutsch, Karl W. 1963. *The Nerves of Government: Models of Political Communication and Control.* New York: Free Press.

Deutsch, Karl W., et al. 1957. *Political Community and the North Atlantic Area.* Princeton, N.J.: Princeton University Press.

Deutsch, Karl W., and Richard L. Merritt. 1965. Effects of events on national and international images. In *International Behavior: A Social-Psycho-*

logical Analysis, ed. Herbert Kelman. New York: Holt, Rinehart and Winston.

Divine, Robert A. 1974. *Foreign Policy and U.S. Presidential Elections: 1940–1948.* New York: New Viewpoints.

Domke, William. 1988. *War and the Changing Global System.* New Haven, Conn.: Yale University Press.

Domke, William, Richard Eichenberg, and Catherine Kelleher. 1987. Consensus lost? Domestic politics and the "crisis" in NATO. *World Politics* 39(3): 382–407.

Downey, Thomas J. 1984. On Congress and security. *World Policy Journal* 1: 447–460.

Doyle, Michael. 1986. Liberalism and world politics. *American Political Science Review* 80(4): 1151–1161.

Duroselle, Jean-Baptiste. 1988. Western Europe and the impossible war. *Journal of International Affairs* 41(2): 345–361.

Edwards, George C., III. 1980. *Presidential Influence in Congress.* New York: W. H. Freeman.

——— 1983. *The Public Presidency: The Pursuit of Popular Support.* New York: St. Martin's.

Eichenberg, Richard. 1989. Strategy and consensus: Public support for military policy in industrial democracies. In *National Security and Arms Control: A Guide to Policy Making,* ed. Edward Kolodziej and Patrick Morgan. Westport, Conn.: Greenwood.

Elder, Robert, and Jack Holmes. 1988. Prosperity, consensus, and assertive foreign policy: A long-term analysis of historical relationships in American foreign policy. Paper presented at the annual meeting of the International Studies Association, St. Louis.

Epstein, Edward J. 1983. The cartel that never was. *Atlantic Monthly,* March, 70–75.

Erikson, Robert S. 1978a. Constituency opinion and congressional behavior: A reexamination of the Miller-Stokes representation data. *Public Opinion Quarterly* 42: 510–35.

——— 1978b. Analyzing one-variable three-wave panel data: A comparison of the two models. *Political Methodology* 5: 151–161.

——— 1979. The SRC political data and mass political attitudes. *British Journal of Political Science* 9(1): 89–114.

Erskine, Hazel Gaudet. 1963. The polls: Atomic weapons and nuclear energy. *Public Opinion Quarterly* 27(2): 155–190.

——— 1970. The polls: Is war a mistake? *Public Opinion Quarterly* 34: 134–150.

Etheredge, Lloyd. 1978. *A World of Men: The Private Sources of American Foreign Policy.* Cambridge, Mass.: M.I.T. Press.

Etzioni, Amitai. 1967. The Kennedy experiment. *Western Political Quarterly* 20: 361–380.

Eurobarometre: Public Opinion in the European Community. 1986. Vol. 25 (June).

Evarts, Philip P. 1989. The peace movement and public opinion: Prospects for the nineties. Paper prepared for the annual meeting of the International Studies Association, London.

Fagen, Richard R. 1960. Some assessments and uses of public opinion in diplomacy. *Public Opinion Quarterly* 24: 448–457.

Falk, Richard. 1981. *Human Rights and State Sovereignty.* New York: Holmes and Meier.

Fan, David P. 1988. *Predictions of Public Opinion from the Mass Media: Computer Content Analysis and Mathematical Modelling.* Westport, Conn.: Greenwood.

Feshback, S., and M. J. White. 1986. Individual differences in attitudes toward nuclear arms policies. *Journal of Peace Research* 23: 129–140.

Fiorina, Morris. 1981. *Retrospective Voting in American National Elections.* New Haven, Conn.: Yale University Press.

Fliess, Peter J. 1966. *Thucydides and the Politics of Bipolarity.* Nashville, Tenn.: Parthenon Press for Louisiana State University Press.

Florini, Ann. 1988. The opening skies: Third-party imaging satellites and U.S. security. *International Security* 13(2): 91–123.

Flynn, Gregory, Edwina Moreton, and Gregory Treverton. 1985. *Public Images of Western Security.* Paris: Atlantic Institute for International Affairs.

Flynn, Gregory, and Hans Rattinger, eds. 1985. *The Public and Atlantic Defense.* Totowa, N.J.: Rowman and Allanheld.

Foreign Opinion Note. 1989. Washington, D.C.: U.S. Information Agency, April 28.

Free, Lloyd, and Albert Cantril. 1967. *The Political Beliefs of Americans: A Study of Public Opinion.* New Brunswick, N.J.: Rutgers University Press.

Free, Lloyd, and William Watts. 1980. Internationalism comes of age . . . again. *Public Opinion* 3: 46–50.

Freeman, John R., and Joshua S. Goldstein. 1989. U.S.–Soviet–Chinese relations: Routine, reciprocity, or rational expectations? Paper prepared for the annual meeting of the International Studies Association, London.

Gallup Report (previously *Gallup Opinion*). Various issues.

Galtung, Johan. 1967. Social position, party identification, and foreign policy orientation: A Norwegian case study. In *Domestic Sources of Foreign Policy*, ed. James N. Rosenau. New York: Free Press.

Gamson, William, and Andre Modigliani. 1966. Knowledge and foreign policy options: Some models for consideration. *Public Opinion Quarterly* 30: 187–199.

—— 1989. Media discourse and public opinion: A constructionist approach, *American Journal of Sociology* 95(1): 1–37.

Gantzel, Klaus Juergen. 1987. Is democracy a guarantor against war-making policy? Working Paper no. 14. University of Hamburg, Institut fur Politische Wissenschaft, Center for the Study of Wars, Armaments, and Development.

Gasiorowski, Mark, and Solomon Polachek. 1982. Conflict and interdependence: East-West trade and linkages in the era of détente. *Journal of Conflict Resolution* 26(4): 709–729.

Gastil, Raymond. 1988. *Freedom in the World: Political Rights and Civil Liberties, 1987–1988*. New York: Freedom House.

—— 1989. *Freedom in the World: Political Rights and Civil Liberties, 1988–1989*. New York: Freedom House.

Gaubatz, Kurt Taylor. 1989. Elections and war. Paper presented at the annual meeting of the American Political Science Association, Atlanta.

Gergen, David R. 1980. The hardening mood towards foreign policy. *Public Opinion* 3: 12–13.

Goldmann, Kjell, Sten Berglund, and Gunnar Sjöstedt. 1986. *Democracy and Foreign Policy: The Case of Sweden*. Aldershot, Hampshire: Gower.

Goldstein, Joshua. 1988. *Long Cycles: Prosperity and War in the Modern Age*. New Haven, Conn.: Yale University Press.

Gordon, Michael R. 1974. Domestic conflict and the origins of the First World War: The British and German cases. *Journal of Modern History* 46(2): 191–226.

Graham, Thomas W. 1986. *Public Attitudes toward Active Defense: ABM and Star Wars, 1945–1985*. Cambridge, Mass.: Center for International Studies, M.I.T.

—— 1988. The pattern and importance of public awareness and knowledge in the nuclear age. *Journal of Conflict Resolution* 32(2): 319–333.

—— 1989a. The politics of failure: Strategic nuclear arms control, public opinion, and domestic politics in the United States, 1945–1985. Ph.D. dissertation, M.I.T.

—— 1989b. American public opinion on NATO, extended deterrence, and use of nuclear weapons: Future fission? Occasional Paper no. 4. Center for Science and International Affairs, Harvard University.

Graham, Thomas W., and Bernard M. Kramer. 1986. The polls: ABM and Star Wars: Attitudes toward nuclear defense, 1945–1985. *Public Opinion Quarterly* 50(1): 125–134.

Gurr, Ted Robert. 1988. War, revolution, and the growth of the coercive state. *Comparative Political Studies* 21(1): 45–65.

Guttman, Louis. 1978. *The Israeli Public, Peace and Territory: The Impact of the Sadat Initiative*. Jerusalem: Jerusalem Institute for Federal Studies.

Hahn, Harlan. 1970. Correlates of public sentiments about war: Local referenda on the Vietnam issue. *American Political Science Review* 64(4): 1186–1198.

Hamilton, Richard F. 1968. A research note on the mass support for "tough" military initiatives. *American Sociological Review* 33: 439–445.

Hanson, Eric. 1987. *The Catholic Church in World Politics*. Princeton, N.J.: Princeton University Press.

Haskell, Thomas L. 1987. The curious persistence of rights talk in the "age of interpretation." *American Historical Review* 74(3): 984–1012.

Hendershott, Patric, and Joseph Peek. 1987. Private saving in the United

States: 1950–1985. National Bureau of Economic Research Working Paper no. 2294.

Hertsgaard, Mark. 1988 *On Bended Knee: The Press and the Reagan Presidency.* New York: Farrar, Straus, and Giroux.

Hibbs, Douglas. 1987. *The Political Economy of Industrial Democracies.* Cambridge, Mass.: Harvard University Press.

Hinckley, Ronald H. 1988a. Polls and peacemakers: The case of the National Security Council. Paper presented at the annual meeting of the American Association for Public Opinion Research, Toronto.

—— 1988b. Public attitudes toward key foreign policy events. *Journal of Conflict Resolution* 32(2): 295–318.

—— 1990. American opinion toward the Soviet Union. *International Journal for Public Opinion Research,* forthcoming.

Holsti, Ole. 1986. Public opinion and containment. In *Containment: Concept and Policy,* ed. Terry L. Deibel and John Lewis Gaddis. Washington, D.C.: National Defense University Press.

—— 1988. American public opinion on the Soviet Union. Paper prepared for the annual meeting of the American Political Science Association, Washington, D.C.

Holsti, Ole, and James N. Rosenau. 1984. *American Leadership in World Affairs.* Boston: Allen and Unwin.

—— 1986. Consensus lost, consensus regained? Foreign policy beliefs of American leaders, 1976–1980. *International Studies Quarterly* 30(3): 375–409.

—— 1988. Domestic and foreign policy belief systems among American leaders. *Journal of Conflict Resolution* 32(2): 248–294.

Hughes, Barry. 1978. *The Domestic Context of American Foreign Policy.* New York: Freeman.

Hurwitz, Jon, and Mark Peffley. 1987. How are foreign policy attitudes structured? A hierarchical model. *American Political Science Review* 81(4): 1099–1120.

Huth, Paul, and Bruce Russett. 1988. Deterrence failure and crisis escalation. *International Studies Quarterly* 32(1): 29–45.

Hyman, Herbert. 1972. *Secondary Analysis of Sample Surveys.* New York: Wiley.

Inbar, Michael, and Ephraim Yuchtman-Yaar. 1989. The people's image of conflict resolution: Israelis and Palestinians. *Journal of Conflict Resolution* 33(1): 37–66.

Iyengar, Shanto, and Donald R. Kinder. 1987. *News That Matters: Television and American Opinion.* Chicago: University of Chicago Press.

Jacobson, Gary C. 1983. *The Politics of Congressional Elections.* Boston: Little, Brown.

Jacobson, Harold K. 1985. *The Determination of the United States Military Force Posture: Political Processes and Policy Changes.* Washington, D.C.: International Security Program, Woodrow Wilson Center.

James, Patrick. 1987. Externalization of conflict: Testing a crisis-based model. *Canadian Journal of Political Science* 20: 573–598.

——— 1988. *Crisis and War.* Montreal and Kingston: McGill–Queen's University Press.

Jangotch, Nish, ed. 1985. *Sectors of Mutual Benefit in U.S.–Soviet Relations.* Durham, N.C.: Duke University Press.

Janis, Irving, and Ralph Mann. 1977. *Decision Making.* New York: Free Press.

Jensen, Lloyd. 1982. *Explaining Foreign Policy.* Englewood Cliffs, N.J.: Prentice-Hall.

Jervis, Robert. 1976. *Perception and Misperception in International Politics.* Princeton, N.J.: Princeton University Press.

Kahneman, Daniel, and Amos Tversky. 1979. Prospect theory: An analysis of decision under risk. *Econometrica* 47(2): 263–292.

Katz, Andrew. 1988. Who ended the Vietnam war? Manuscript. Gambier, Ohio: Kenyon College, Political Science Department.

Katz, Elihu. 1989. Hawkish majority, but dovish trend. *Jerusalem Post,* February 10, 4.

Katz, Elihu, and Paul F. Lazarsfeld. 1955. *Personal Influence.* New York: Free Press.

Katz, Elihu, Martin Levin, and Herbert Hamilton. 1963. Traditions of research on the diffusion of innovation. *American Sociological Review* 28(2): 237–252.

Kelman, Steven. 1987. *Making Public Policy: A Hopeful View of American Government.* New York: Basic Books.

Keohane, Robert O. 1984. *After Hegemony: Cooperation and Discord in the World Political Economy.* Princeton, N.J.: Princeton University Press.

Kern, Montague, Patricia Levering, and Ralph Levering. 1983. *The Kennedy Crises: The Press, the Presidency, and Foreign Policy.* Chapel Hill: University of North Carolina Press.

Kernell, Samuel. 1978. Explaining presidential popularity. *American Political Science Review* 72: 506–522.

——— 1986. *Going Public: New Strategies of Presidential Leadership.* Washington, D.C.: Congressional Quarterly.

Kiewiet, D. Roderick. 1983. *Macroeconomics and Micropolitics.* Chicago: University of Chicago Press.

Kim, Samuel S. 1984. *The Quest for a Just World Order.* Boulder, Colo: Westview.

Kinder, Donald R. 1981. Presidents, prosperity, and public opinion. *Public Opinion Quarterly* 45(1): 1–21.

Kinder, Donald R., Gordon S. Adams, and Paul Gronke. 1989. Economics and politics in the 1984 presidential election. *American Journal of Political Science* 33(2): 491–515.

Kindleberger, Charles. 1973. *The World in Depression, 1929–1939.* London: Allen Lane.

Kissinger, Henry. 1979. *White House Years.* Boston: Little, Brown.

Knox, MacGregor. 1984. Conquest, domestic and foreign, in Fascist Italy and Nazi Germany. *Journal of Modern History* 56(1): 1–57.

Kohut, Andrew. 1988. What Americans want. *Foreign Policy* 70 (Spring): 150–166.

Kohut, Andrew, and Nicholas Horrock. 1984. Generally speaking: Surveying the military's top brass. *Public Opinion* 7(5): 42–45.

Kozyrev, Andrei. 1988. Confidence and the balance of interests. *International Affairs* (Moscow) 1988(11): 3–12.

Kramer, Bernard M., S. Michael Kalick, and Michael Milburn. 1983. Attitudes toward nuclear weapons and nuclear war. *Journal of Social Issues* 39(1): 7–24.

Kramer, Gerald H. 1971. Short-term fluctuations in U.S. voting behavior. *American Political Science Review* 65(1): 131–143.

Krell, Gert. 1981. Capabilities and armaments: Business cycles and defense spending in the United States, 1945–79. *Journal of Peace Research* 18(3): 221–240.

Kriesberg, Louis, and Ross Klein. 1980. Changes in public support for U.S. military spending. *Journal of Conflict Resolution* 24(1): 79–111.

Kusnitz, Leonard. 1984. *Public Opinion and Foreign Policy: America's China Policy, 1949–1979.* Westport, Conn.: Greenwood.

Lake, David A. 1989. Why democratic states win wars: The virtues of political competition. Paper prepared for the annual meeting of the International Studies Association, London.

LaMare, James W. 1987. International conflict: ANZUS and New Zealand public opinion. *Journal of Conflict Resolution* 31(3): 420–437.

Lear, T. J. Jackson. 1985. The concept of cultural hegemony. *American Historical Review* 90(3): 567–594.

Lebow, Richard Ned. 1981. *Between Peace and War.* Baltimore: Johns Hopkins University Press.

—— 1985. Conclusions. In *Psychology and Deterrence,* ed. Robert Jervis, Richard Ned Lebow, and Janice Stein. Baltimore: Johns Hopkins University Press.

Lee, Jong Ryool. 1977. Rally 'round the flag: Foreign policy events and presidential popularity. *Presidential Studies Quarterly* 7: 252–255.

Legvold, Robert. 1988/89. The revolution in Soviet foreign policy. *Foreign Affairs* 68(1): 82–98.

Leigh, Michael. 1976. *Mobilizing Consent: Public Opinion and American Foreign Policy, 1937–1947.* Westport, Conn.: Greenwood.

Leng, Russell. 1984. Reagan and the Russians: Crisis bargaining beliefs and the historical record. *American Political Science Review* 78(2): 655–684.

LeVine, Robert A., and Donald T. Campbell. 1972. *Ethnocentrism: Theories of Conflict, Ethnic Attitudes, and Group Behavior.* New York: Wiley.

Levy, Jack S. 1989. The diversionary theory of war: A critique. In *Handbook of War Studies,* ed. Manus Midlarsky. London: Unwin Hyman.

Levy, Jack S., and Lily Vakili. 1989. External scapegoating by authoritarian regimes: Argentina in the Falklands/Malvinas case. Paper prepared for the annual meeting of the American Political Science Association, Atlanta.

Lewis-Beck, Michael S. 1985. Une modele de prevision des elections legislatives françaises (avec une application pour 1986). *Revue Française de Science Politique* 35(6): 1080–1091.

Lifton, Robert, and Richard Falk. 1982. *Indefensible Weapons: The Political and Psychological Case against Nuclearism.* New York: Basic Books.

Lindblom, C. E. 1977. *Politics and Markets: The World's Political-Economic Systems.* New York: Basic Books.

Lindsay, James M. 1986. Trade sanctions as policy instruments: A reexamination. *International Studies Quarterly* 30(2): 153–174.

Lowi, Theodore J. 1985. *The Personal President.* Ithaca, N.Y.: Cornell University Press.

Lunch, William L., and Peter Sperlich. 1979. American public opinion and the war in Vietnam. *Western Political Quarterly* 32:21–44.

Luttwak, Edward. 1987. *Strategy: The Logic of War and Peace.* Cambridge, Mass.: Harvard University Press.

MacDougal, Myres, Harold Lasswell, and Lung-chu Chen. 1980. *Human Rights and World Public Order.* New Haven, Conn.: Yale University Press.

Macfie, A. L. 1938. The outbreak of war and the trade cycle. *Economic History* 3(1): 89–97.

McGuire, William. 1969. The nature of attitudes and attitude change. In *Handbook of Social Psychology,* ed. G. Lindzey and E. Aronson, 2nd. ed., vol. 3. Reading, Mass.: Addison Wesley.

Mack, John E. 1981. Psychological aspects of the nuclear arms race. *Bulletin of the Atomic Scientists* 37 (4): 18–23.

Mack, John E., and Roberta Snow. 1986. Psychological effects on children and adolescents. In *Psychology and the Prevention of Nuclear War,* ed. Ralph K. White. New York: New York University Press.

MacKuen, Michael B. 1983. Political drama, economic conditions, and the dynamics of presidential popularity. *American Journal of Political Science* 27(2): 165–192.

Mandel, Robert. 1989. Public opinion and superpower strategic arms. Paper prepared for the annual meeting of the International Studies Association, London.

Mandelbaum, Michael, and William Schneider. 1979. The new internationalism: Public opinion and American foreign policy. In *Eagle Entangled: U.S. Foreign Policy in a Complex World,* ed. Kenneth Oye, Donald Rothchild, and Robert Lieber. New York: Longman.

Mansfield, Edward D. 1988. The distribution of wars over time. *World Politics* 41(1): 21–51.

Mansfield, Harvey, Jr. 1983. On the impersonality of the modern state. *American Political Science Review* 77(4): 849–857.

Maoz, Zeev, and Nasrin Abdolali. 1989. Regime types and international ccnflict, 1816–1976. *Journal of Conflict Resolution* 29(1): 3–35.

Marra, Robin, and Charles Ostrom. 1989. Explaining seat change in the U.S. House of Representatives, 1950–1986. *American Journal of Political Science* 31(3): 541–569.

Marra, Robin, Charles Ostrom, and Dennis Simon. 1989. *Foreign policy in the perpetual election: Presidential popularity, foreign policy, and windows of opportunity.* Paper prepared for the annual meeting of the International Studies Association, London.

Martilla, John. 1989. American public opinion: Evolving definitions of national security. In *America's Global Interests: A New Agenda,* ed. Edward K. Hamilton. New York: Norton.

Mayer, Arno. 1977. Internal crisis and war since 1870. In *Revolutionary Situations in Europe, 1917–1922,* ed. C. L. Bertrand. Montreal: McGill University Press.

Mayer, Kenneth E. 1991. *The Politics and Economics of Defense Contracting.* New Haven, Conn.: Yale University Press.

Milburn, Michael, Paul Watanabe, and Bernard Kramer. 1986. The nature and sources of attitudes toward a nuclear freeze. *Political Psychology* 7(4): 661–674.

Miller, Nicholas R. 1977. Pluralism and social choice. *American Political Science Review* 77(3): 734–747.

Miller, Warren. 1964. Majority rule and the representative system of government. In *Cleavages, Ideologies, and Party Systems,* ed. E. Allardt and Y. Littunen. Helsinki: Transactions of the Westermarck Society.

Miller, Warren, and Donald Stokes. 1966. Constituency influence in Congress. In *Elections and the Political Order,* ed. Angus Campbell, Philip Converse, Warren Miller, and Donald Stokes. New York: Wiley.

Mills, C. Wright. 1956. *The Power Elite.* New York: Oxford University Press.

Mintz, Alex. 1988a. *The Politics of Resource Allocation in the U.S. Department of Defense: International Crises and Domestic Constraints.* Boulder, Colo: Westview.

——— 1988b. Electoral cycles and defense spending: A comparison of Israel and the United States. *Comparative Political Studies* 21(3): 368–382.

Mintz, Alex, and A. M. Hicks. 1984. Military Keynesianism in the United States, 1949–1976: Disaggregating military expenditures and their determination. *American Journal of Sociology* 90(2): 411–417.

Mintz, Alex, and Michael D. Ward. 1988. The evolution of Israel's military expenditures: 1960–1983. *Western Political Quarterly* 41(3): 489–507.

——— 1989. The political economy of military spending in Israel. *American Political Science Review* 83(2): 521–534.

Miroff, Bruce. 1976. *Pragmatic Illusions: The Presidential Politics of John F. Kennedy.* New York: David McKay.

Modelski, George. 1988. *Is America's Decline Inevitable?* Uhlenbeck-Lecture, no. 6. Wassenaar: Netherlands Institute for Advanced Study.

Modigliani, Andre. 1972. Hawks and doves: Isolationism and political distrust. *American Political Science Review* 66(3): 960–978.

Monroe, Alan D. 1979. Consistency between public preferences and national policy decisions. *American Politics Quarterly* 7(1): 3–19.

Monroe, Kristen. 1984. *Presidential Popularity and the Economy.* New York: Praeger.

Morgan, T. Clifton, and Kenneth Bickers. 1989. Domestic politics and aggressive foreign policy: A causal link? Paper presented at the annual meeting of the American Political Science Association, Atlanta.

Morin, Richard. 1988. Democrats, GOP aligning on Soviets. *Washington Post*, January 30, 9.

Moyers, Bill D. 1968. One thing we learned. *Foreign Affairs* 46: 657–664.

Mueller, Harold, and Thomas Risse-Kappen. 1987. Origins of estrangement: The peace movement and the changed image of America in Germany. *International Security* 12(1): 52–88.

Mueller, John E. 1973. *War, Presidents, and Public Opinion.* New York: Wiley.

——— 1977. Changes in American public attitudes toward international involvement. In *The Limits of Military Intervention*, ed. Ellen Stern. Beverly Hills, Calif.: Sage.

——— 1979. Public expectations of war during the cold war. *American Journal of Political Science* 23(2): 301–329.

——— 1989. *Retreat from Doomsday: The Obsolescence of Major War.* New York: Basic Books.

Munton, Don. 1984. Public opinion and the media in Canada from cold war to détente to new cold war. *International Journal* 39: 171–213.

Natchez, Peter. 1985. *Images of Voting/Visions of Democracy.* New York: Basic Books.

Neuman, W. Russell. 1986. *The Paradox of Mass Politics: Knowledge and Opinion in the American Electorate.* Cambridge, Mass.: Harvard University Press.

Neustadt, Richard. 1980. *Presidential Power.* 3rd ed. New York: John Wiley.

Nincic, Miroslav. 1988a. The United States, the Soviet Union, and the politics of opposites. *World Politics* 40: 452–475.

——— 1988b. *U.S. Foreign Policy.* Washington, D.C: Congressional Quarterly.

——— 1990. U.S. Soviet policy and the electoral connection. *World Politics* 42(3).

Nincic, Miroslav, and Thomas Cusack. 1979. The political economy of U.S. military spending. *Journal of Peace Research* 16(2): 101–115.

Nincic, Miroslav, and Barbara Hinckley. 1990. Foreign policy and presidential elections. Forthcoming.

Nincic, Miroslav, and Bruce Russett. 1979. The effect of similarity and interest on attitudes toward foreign countries. *Public Opinion Quarterly* 33(1): 68–78.

Noelle-Neumann, Elisabeth. 1984. *The Spiral of Silence: Public Opinion and Our Social Skin.* Chicago: University of Chicago Press.

Nordhaus, William. 1975. The political business cycle. *Review of Economic Studies* 42(1): 169–189.

Norpoth, Helmut. 1987. Guns and butter and government popularity in Britain. *American Political Science Review* 81(3): 449–460.

Nye, Joseph R., Jr. 1988. Neorealism and neoliberalism, *World Politics* 40(2): 235–251.

O'Donnell, Guillermo. 1988. Challenges to democratization in Brazil. *World Policy Journal* 5(2): 281–300.

Osgood, Charles E. 1962. *An Alternative to War or Surrender.* Urbana: University of Illinois Press.

Ostrom, Charles W., and Brian Job. 1986. The president and the political use of force. *American Political Science Review* 80(2): 541–566.

Ostrom, Charles W., and Robin Marra. 1986. U.S. defense spending and the Soviet estimate. *American Political Science Review* 80(3): 819–842.

Ostrom, Charles W., and Dennis Simon. 1985. Promise and performance: A dynamic model of presidential popularity. *American Political Science Review* 79: 334–358.

———— 1988. The president's public. *American Journal of Political Science* 32(4): 1096–1119.

Page, Benjamin I., and Robert Y. Shapiro. 1983. Effects of public opinion on policy. *American Political Science Review* 77(1): 175–190.

———— 1984. Presidents as opinion leaders: some new evidence. *Policy Studies Journal* 12(4): 649–661.

———— Forthcoming. *The Rational Public: Fifty Years of Opinion Trends.*

Page, Benjamin I., Robert Y. Shapiro, and Glenn R. Dempsey. 1987. What moves public opinion? *American Political Science Review* 81(1): 23–44.

Page, Benjamin I., Robert Y. Shapiro, Paul Gronke, and Robert Rosenberg. 1984. Constituency, party, and representation in Congress. *Public Opinion Quarterly* 48: 741–756.

Parry, Robert, and Peter Kornbluh. 1988. Iran-Contra's untold story. *Foreign Policy* 72: 1–30.

Paterson, Thomas G. 1988. *Meeting the Communist Threat: Truman to Reagan.* New York: Oxford University Press.

Plous, Scott. 1988. Disarmament, arms control, and peace in the nuclear age: Political objectives and relevant research. *Journal of Social Issues* 44(2): 133–54.

Powlick, Philip J. 1989. American foreign policy and public opinion: The case of Lebanon, 1982–1984. Manuscript. Pittsburgh: University of Pittsburgh, Political Science Department.

Public Agenda Foundation and Brown University Center for Foreign Policy Development. 1988. *The Public, The Soviets and Nuclear Arms: A Mandate for the Future.* New York and Providence: Public Agenda Foundation and Brown University.

Quandt, William. 1986. *Camp David: Peacemaking and Politics.* Washington, D.C.: Brookings Institution.

Rattinger, Hans. 1987. Change and continuity in West German public attitudes on national security and nuclear weapons in the 1980s. *Public Opinion Quarterly* 51(4): 495–521.

Reilly, John E., ed. 1983. *American Public Opinion and U.S. Foreign Policy.* Chicago: Chicago Council on Foreign Relations.

————, ed. 1987. *American Public Opinion and U.S. Foreign Policy, 1987.* Chicago: Chicago Council on Foreign Relations.

Riker, William H. 1984. *Liberalism against Populism: A Confrontation between the Theory of Democracy and the Theory of Social Choice.* New York: W. H. Freeman.

Robinson, John P., and Robert Meadow. 1982. *Polls Apart.* Washington, D.C.: Seven Locks Press.

Rock, Stephen R. 1989. *Why Peace Breaks Out: Great Power Rapprochement in Historical Perspective.* Chapel Hill: University of North Carolina Press.

Rose, Richard. 1985. Can the president steer the American economy? *Journal of Public Policy* 5: 267–280.

——— 1988. *The Post-Modern President: The White House Meets the World.* Chatham, N.J.: Chatham House.

Rosecrance, Richard. 1986. *The Rise of the Trading State.* New York: Basic Books.

Rummel, R. J. 1983. Libertarianism and international violence. *Journal of Conflict Resolution* 27(1): 27–71.

——— 1985. Libertarian propositions on violence within and between nations. *Journal of Conflict Resolution* 29(3): 419–455.

Russett, Bruce. 1963. *Community and Contention: Britain and America in the Twentieth Century.* Cambridge, Mass.: M.I.T. Press.

——— 1968. *International Regions and the International System.* Chicago: Rand McNally.

——— 1974. The revolt of the masses: Public opinion toward military expenditures. In *The New Civil-Military Relations,* ed. J. Lovell and P. Kronnenberg. New Brunswick, N.J.: Transaction.

——— 1983a. International interactions and processes: The internal-external debate revisited. In *Political Science: The State of the Discipline,* ed. Ada Finifter. Washington, D.C.: American Political Science Association.

——— 1983b. *The Prisoners of Insecurity: Nuclear Deterrence, the Arms Race, and Arms Control.* New York: W. H. Freeman.

——— 1989. Democracy, public opinion, and nuclear weapons. In *Behavior, Society, and Nuclear War,* ed. Philip Tetlock, Jo Husbands, Robert Jervis, Philip Stern, and Charles Tilly. New York: Oxford University Press.

——— 1990. Economic decline, electoral pressure, and the initiation of interstate conflict. In *Prisoners of War? Nation-States in the Modern Era,* ed. Charles Gochman and Alan Ned Sabrosky. Lexington, Mass.: D. C. Heath.

Russett, Bruce, and Donald R. DeLuca. 1981. Don't tread on me: Public opinion and foreign policy in the eighties. *Political Science Quarterly* 96(3): 381–399.

——— 1983. Theater nuclear forces: Public opinion in Western Europe. *Political Science Quarterly* 98(2): 179–196.

Russett, Bruce, and Elizabeth C. Hanson. 1975. *Interest and Ideology: The Foreign Policy Beliefs of American Businessmen.* New York: W. H. Freeman.

Russett, Bruce, and Miles Lackey. 1987. In the shadow of the cloud: If there's no tomorrow, why save today? *Political Science Quarterly* 102(2): 259–272.

Russett, Bruce, and Samuel Shye. 1990. Aggressiveness, involvement, and determination as dimensions of foreign policy attitudes: Assessment by multiple scaling. Forthcoming.

Russett, Bruce, and Harvey Starr. 1989. *World Politics: The Menu for Choice.* 3rd ed. New York: W. H. Freeman.

Russett, Cynthia Eagle. 1989. *Sexual Science: The Victorian Construction of Womanhood.* Cambridge, Mass.: Harvard University Press.

Sabin, Philip A. G. 1986. *The Third World War Scare in Britain: A Critical Analysis.* London: Macmillan.

——— 1986/87. Proposals and propaganda: Arms control and British public opinion in the 1980s. *International Affairs* 63(1): 49–63.

Sachar, Howard M. 1987. *A History of Israel.* Vol. 2: *From the Aftermath of the Yom Kippur War.* New York: Oxford University Press.

Sanders, David, Hugh Ward, and David Marsh (with Tony Fletcher). 1987. Government popularity and the Falklands war: A reassessment. *British Journal of Political Science* 17(3): 287–314.

Sartori, Giovanni. 1987. *The Theory of Democracy Revisited.* Chatham, N.J.: Chatham House.

Schneider, William. 1984. Public opinion. In *The Making of America's Soviet Policy,* ed. Joseph Nye. New Haven, Conn.: Yale University Press.

——— 1987. Rambo and reality: Having it both ways. In *Eagle Resurgent? The Reagan Era in American Foreign Policy,* ed. Kenneth Oye, Robert Lieber, and Donald Rothchild. Boston: Little, Brown.

Schuman, Howard, Jacob Ludwig, and Jon Krosnick. 1986. The perceived threat of nuclear war, salience, and open questions. *Public Opinion Quarterly* 50(4): 519–536.

Senghaas, Dieter. 1972. *Rüstung und Militarismus.* Frankfurt am Main: Suhrkampf.

Shapiro, Robert Y., and Harpreet Mahajan. 1986. Gender differences in policy preferences. *Public Opinion Quarterly* 50(1): 46–61.

Shapiro, Robert Y., and Benjamin I. Page. 1988. Foreign policy and the rational public. *Journal of Conflict Resolution* 32(2): 211–247.

Shaw, R. Paul, and Yuwa Wong. 1988. *Genetic Seeds of Warfare: Evolution, Nationalism, and Patriotism.* Boston: Unwin Hyman.

Sigelman, Lee. 1980. Gauging the public response to presidential leadership. *Presidential Studies Quarterly* 10: 427–433.

Simonton, Dean Keith. 1987. *Why Presidents Succeed: A Political Psychology of Leadership.* New Haven, Conn.: Yale University Press.

Shue, Henry. 1980. *Basic Rights: Subsistence, Affluence, and U.S. Foreign Policy.* Princeton, N.J.: Princeton University Press.

Slemrod, Joel. 1986. Savings and the fear of nuclear war. *Journal of Conflict Resolution* 30(3): 403–419.

Small, Jeffrey P. 1989. Public attitudes toward building nuclear weapons and nuclear deterrence. Senior Essay, Yale University.

Small, Melvin, and J. David Singer. 1976. The war-proneness of democratic regimes. *Jerusalem Journal of International Relations* 1(1): 50–69.

Small, Melvin, and J. David Singer. 1982. *Resort to Arms: International and Civil Wars, 1816–1980.* Beverly Hills, Calif.: Sage.

Smith, Robert B. 1971. Disaffection, delegitimation, and consequences: Aggregate trends for World War II, Korea, and Vietnam. In *Public Opinion and the Military Establishment,* ed. Charles C. Moskos, Jr. Beverly Hills, Calif: Sage.

Smith, Tom W. 1984. The polls: Gender and attitudes toward violence. *Public Opinion Quarterly* 48(1): 384–396.

———— 1985. The polls: America's most important problem, part I: national and international. *Public Opinion Quarterly* 49(2): 264–274.

———— 1988. Report: Nuclear anxiety. *Public Opinion Quarterly* 52(4): 557–575.

Smith, Tom W., and Michael Hogan. 1987. Public opinion and the Panama Canal treaties of 1977. *Public Opinion Quarterly* 51(1): 5–30.

Sniderman, Paul M., and Philip E. Tetlock. 1986. Interrelationship of political ideology and public opinion. In *Political Psychology,* ed. Margaret E. Hermann. San Francisco: Jossey-Bass.

Steele, Ronald. 1978. American public opinion and the war against Germany: The issue of negotiated peace—1942. *Journal of American History* 65: 704–723.

Stein, Arthur. 1980. *The Nation at War.* Baltimore: Johns Hopkins University Press.

Stein, Arthur, and Bruce Russett. 1980. Evaluating war: outcomes and consequences. In *Handbook of Political Conflict: Theory and Research,* ed. Ted Robert Gurr. New York: Free Press.

Stohl, Michael. 1975. War and domestic political violence: The case of the United States, 1890–1970. *Journal of Conflict Resolution* 19: 379–416.

———— 1980. The nexus of civil and international conflict. In *Handbook of Political Conflict,* ed. Ted Robert Gurr. New York: Free Press.

Stoll, Richard J. 1984. The guns of November: Presidential reelections and the use of force. *Journal of Conflict Resolution* 28(2): 231–246.

———— 1987. The sound of guns: Is there a congressional rally effect after U.S. military action? *American Politics Quarterly* 15(2): 223–237.

Stone, Russell A. 1982. *Social Change in Israel: Attitudes and Events, 1967–79.* New York: Praeger.

Suedfeld, Peter, and Philip Tetlock. 1977. Integrative complexity and communication in international crises. *Journal of Conflict Resolution* 21(1): 169–184.

Tetlock, Philip. 1985. Integrative complexity of American and Soviet foreign policy rhetoric. *Journal of Personality and Social Psychology* 49(6): 1565–1585.

Tetlock, Philip, and C. McGuire. 1985. Integrative complexity as a predictor of Soviet foreign policy behavior. *International Journal of Group Tensions* 14: 113–128.

Thompson, William R. 1982. Phases of the business cycle and the outbreak of war. *International Studies Quarterly* 26(2): 301–311.

Thompson, William R., and Gary Zuk. 1982. American elections and the international economic cycle. *Journal of Conflict Resolution* 26(3): 464–484.

Tilly, Charles. 1985. War making and state making as organized crime. In *Bringing the State Back In*, ed. Peter Evans, Dieter Rueschmeyer, and Theda Skocpol. Cambridge: Cambridge University Press.

Tocqueville, Alexis de. 1945. *Democracy in America*. 2 vols. New York: Knopf.

Tufte, Edward R. 1978. *Political Control of the Economy*. Princeton, N.J.: Princeton University Press.

Tulis, Jeffrey K. 1987. *The Rhetorical Presidency*. Princeton, N.J.: Princeton University Press.

Tyler, T. R., and K. M. McGraw. 1983. The threat of nuclear war: Risk interpretation and behavioral response. *Journal of Social Issues* 39(1): 25–40.

Vasquez, John. 1988. The steps to war: Toward a scientific explanation of correlates of war findings. *World Politics* 40(1): 108–145.

Verba, Sidney, Richard Brody, Edwin Parker, Norman Nie, Nelson Polsby, Paul Ekman, and Gordon Black. 1967. Public opinion and the war in Vietnam. *American Political Science Review* 61(2): 313–333.

Vincent, R. J. 1984. Racial equality. In *The Expansion of International Society*, ed. Hedley Bull and Adam Watson. Oxford: Clarendon.

Volten, Peter M. E. 1982. *Brezhnev's Peace Plan: A Study of Soviet Domestic Political Process and Power*. Boulder, Colo: Westview.

Wallensteen, Peter. 1973. *Structure and War: On International Relations, 1920–1968*. Stockholm: Raben and Sjogren.

Waltz, Kenneth. 1979. *Theory of International Relations*. Reading, Mass.: Addison Wesley.

Ward, Michael D. 1984. Differential paths to parity: A study of the contemporary arms race. *American Political Science Review* 78(2): 297–317.

Weart, Spencer R. 1988. *Nuclear Fear: A History*. Cambridge, Mass.: Harvard University Press.

Weede, Erich. 1984. Democracy and war involvement. *Journal of Conflict Resolution* 28(4): 649–664.

Weissberg, Robert. 1976. *Public Opinion and Popular Government*. Englewood Cliffs, N.J.: Prentice-Hall.

Westerfield, H. Bradford. 1955. *Foreign Policy and Party Politics: Pearl Harbor to Korea*. New Haven: Yale University Press.

Weston, Burns, Robin Lukes, and Kelly Hnatt. 1987. Regional human rights regimes: A comparison and appraisal. *Vanderbilt Journal of Transnational Law* 20(4): 585–637.

Wilkinson, David. 1980. *Deadly Quarrels: Lewis F. Richardson and the Statistical Study of War*. Berkeley: University of California Press.

Withey, Stephen B. 1954. *Fourth Survey of Public Knowledge and Attitudes Concerning Civil Defense*. Ann Arbor, Mich.: Institute for Social Research.

Wittkopf, Eugene. 1986. On the foreign policy beliefs of the American people: A critique and some evidence. *International Studies Quarterly* 30(4): 425–445.

—— 1987. Elites and masses: Another look at attitudes toward America's role. *International Studies Quarterly* 31(2): 131–159.

Wittkopf, Eugene, and Michael Maggiotto. 1983. Elites and masses: A comparative analysis of attitudes toward America's role. *Journal of Politics* 45(2): 307–333.

Yankelovich, Daniel, and John Doble. 1984. The public mood. *Foreign Affairs* 68(1): 33–46.

Yankelovich, Daniel, and Sidney Harman. 1988. *Starting with the People*. Boston: Houghton-Mifflin.

Yankelovich, Daniel, and Richard Smoke. 1988. America's "new thinking." *Foreign Affairs* 67(1): 1–17.

Ziegler, Andrew H. 1987. The structure of Western European attitudes towards Atlantic cooperation: Implications for the western alliance. *British Journal of Political Science* 14(4): 457–477.

Zinnes, Dina. 1980. Why war? Evidence on the outbreak of international conflict. In *Handbook of Political Conflict*, ed. Ted Robert Gurr. New York: Free Press.

Index